KIND
of FOOL

rely

$14ºº

$7⁵⁰

The Lord has called me
to be a new kind of fool
in this world.

FRANCIS of ASSISI

Meditations on Saint Francis

A New Kind of Fool

by

Christopher Coelho OFM

with line drawings by the author

BURNS & OATES   DAVID LOVELL PUBLISHING

First published in Great Britain in 1991
Burns & Oates Ltd., Wellwood, North Farm Road,
Tunbridge Wells, Kent TN2 3DR

First published in Australia by
David Lovell Publishing
Brunswick, Victoria 3056

This edition contains selections from *A New Kind of
Fool: Meditations with a sketch-book and a camera,
and in prose, poetry and song on Saint Francis and
his values*, originally published by Amruthavani,
India, in 1986.

ISBN 0 86012 184 4 (UK)
ISBN 1 86355 017 8 (Aust)

Photoset by Genesis Typesetting, Rochester, Kent
Printed and bound in Great Britain by
Biddles Ltd, Guildford and King's Lynn

Contents

NON-APOLOGY

I WENT to the tomb of Saint Francis to say goodbye. I had come to Assisi a couple of months ago and had lived there trying to savour the place, to drink in its sights, its sounds, its smells, its textures and its tastes, and to collect my thoughts – and more than thoughts – into a book on Saint Francis and some of his values. Yes, another book on Saint Francis, the man about whom more books have been written and are still being written than about any other saint in Christendom.

The following day I was leaving. So I was at the tomb now to take leave of this man who so filled my world. After Christ I cannot think of anyone who has meant more to me, and, quoting François Mauriac, I am forced to say, "for the same reason there is no one whom I have betrayed more". Sitting near that tomb, you cannot help feeling terribly small, terribly inadequate. All your compromises, your betrayals, your double standards, your big talk and small action, all these come before you, trying to break you.

A few years after the death of the saint, Brother Thomas of Celano wrote: "You know, most holy one, how far we lag behind in following your footsteps . . . draw us after you . . . whom you know to be lukewarm with sloth, torpid with weariness and only half-living for our slackness. See how we drag our steps in following you . . . Our eyes are dazzled and smart as we look upon the brilliance of your holiness." Sitting by that tomb you understand what Celano meant.

The tomb is in a crypt underground, and going down into it is like descending into yourself. There, near the dust and bones of Francis of Assisi, you come face to face with your true self. Yet the weight of it does not crush you. There is something about this place that turns on a ruthless searchlight on all you are, without blinding you to confusion, but assuring you that you are accepted and are in the presence of the man who "walked the earth," as Chesterton said, "as the pardon of God . . . whose presence marked the moment when men could be reconciled not only to God, but to nature, and, most difficult of all, to themselves."

It is usually quiet there, and even when it is not, there is a peace about the place that is louder than all the noise that pious pilgrims and chattering tourists make. You can sit there for hours and forget everything else. In fact when you are anywhere near the basilica it is hard to resist the temptation to go down to the crypt and just be there for a while. And when you are there, don't believe your watch; it lies.

I was there now, pondering in the presence of Francis over the task I was engaged in, of putting down on paper something of what he and his vision meant to me – to re-live and record my personal Francis-experience.

This man, Francis, had brought a new vision into my life and for well over a quarter of a century had shaped my attitudes towards everything – from God and Christ to the earth, to bread, to plastic flowers . . . I wanted now to look closely at Francis, and, from his point of view, at all these, and put down what I found.

With the help of those who had written and spoken wisely about him and his charism I wanted to make my own personal pilgrimage into the mountain cave which is the

soul of Francis, guided by the counsel of St Bonaventure
that

> no reading can be of any help without unction,
> no speculation without devotion,
> no investigation without admiration,
> no observation without gladness,
> no industry without piety,
> no knowledge without love,
> no understanding without humility,
> no study without divine grace,
> and no reflection in the soul without the wisdom
> that comes from the Spirit of God.
>
> (*Itinerarium*, Prologue)

Reading, speculation, investigation and the rest are appa-
rently safe areas, but things like unction, devotion,
admiration, piety, love and gladness bring you to slippery
ground. You make yourself terribly vulnerable. But this is
the risk you have to take.

I was thinking these things over, when I noticed an old
woman walk up to the tomb of Francis, buy a candle from
the rack and light it on the candlestand. This was a form of
devotion I had outgrown long ago. I had been taught during
my ecclesiastical training to be careful of sentiments. When
was the last time I lit a candle to a saint or the Madonna? The
candle was for me the eternal symbol of Christian
superstition and misguided religion.

But sitting there before the tomb of Saint Francis, who never
feared his emotions or despised the devotion of the simple,
and who in his own intuitive way knew the meaning of
gesture and symbol and whose life was one ballet of
unrehearsed ritual or one epic poem of live imagery, I found
myself slowly rising from my seat and walking to the candle
rack. I dropped my 100 lire into the box and took a candle.

9

There were dozens of them burning with cheerful innocence on the four candlestands around the tomb, one near each of Francis' four closest disciples buried around him. I had always had a special soft spot for Leo. I went to the candlestand near his tomb, or rather, the one between those of Leo and Francis, which seemed to stand for the glowing friendship and devotion that existed between disciple and master. I lit my candle from the one that had just been placed there by the old woman and placed it by its side.

The shrine was already well, though soberly, lit by the larger lights that shone there, and my candle would bring no new light. If anything, it would only blacken a little more the rugged stones of the low ceiling, already black with the smoke of millions of candles that had burned there through the years. For a few hours after I had left the sanctuary I would know that my candle was still burning as a continuation of my own presence there. And, perhaps, some other pilgrim would light his candle from mine.

As I left the crypt I felt no obligation to anyone to offer a justification or apology for my simple gesture of adding one flame that would last but a few hours and was useful to no one, but one that I could call my own, to that galaxy shining perpetually at the tomb of my father.

It is for the same reason that I am offering no apology for writing this book.

A New Kind of Fool

To be fully alive,
to be holy,
one needs discipline,
artistry
and a little foolishness.

> *Rabbi Abharam Heschel*

A street in Assisi

1 Praise be to you, my Lord, for Brother Francis!

ONE MORNING I took a walk into the city of Assisi from San Damiano, where I was staying, and visited three places where Saint Francis was born. In the course of centuries no less than six or seven places in the town have claimed this honour. Opinions are so divided, it seems to be next to impossible to come to any sort of certainty regarding the spot.

But these wrangles did not bother me for now. In each of the three places that hold the claim today I knelt down and thanked the Lord from the depths of my being for the fact that Francis of Assisi was born into this world. I could have done that in a thousand places.

•   •   •

I was a little boy when Saint Francis entered my life. He came in through the stories my grandmother used to tell us about the son of a rich cloth merchant who gave up everything for the love of God and became a beggar, and was finally marked with the five wounds of Our Lord. In those days beggars walking from door to door were a more common sight in our part of India than nowadays. When they came to your door, they often started by saying some prayer, an Our Father or a Hail Mary (I suppose they said different prayers in the houses of the Hindus and the Muslims). They then said, "For the love of God, please give

13

us something", and when they received alms they always said, "God bless you". I can still remember my childish imagination visualizing Saint Francis as one of them.

From those beggars in their tattered clothes brown with sweat and dust, the image of Francis in me has grown to gigantic stature. In the process I have grown too, and on reflection I find it difficult to imagine how my own growth would have been, had I not, by some inscrutable stroke of mercy, been brought into the shadow of this man.

The Portrait

As I write this he looks at me from a print of Cimabue's portrait of his that hangs on my wall.[1] I had seen it in books and prints for years as I grew up in Franciscan life and had always loved it for its character and power. In 1971 I was in Assisi on the feast of Saint Francis. During the solemn high mass in the basilica when the Italian sermon seemed interminable, I let my eyes wander and suddenly came upon Cimabue's Francis on the wall to my left. It was like running into an old and intimate friend. I did not mind the sermon being long any more; we had plenty of things to talk over. After mass I came back there again and spent a long time.

As Francis gazes down at me from this picture, somehow his eyes seem to fill the whole room. They are anatomically out of proportion to the face, and the distortion seems to give them the ability to pierce and to speak. They don't look *at* you so much as *into* you, and they always have something to say. They gaze out of a face that has seen much struggle in life, but has not been embittered by it, only sweetened. It is the face of a man who is completely at peace with God, with all people and all nature, and with himself. And you can see it is a peace that has been bought dearly, at the price of anguish. I don't know how humility is connected with shoulders, but there is something about his shoulders that seems to suggest that he thinks of himself as the least of all the people in the world, and is only happy about it.

Cimabue was born fourteen years after the death of Saint Francis, and may well have used for his model a portrait of Francis made probably a year before his death and preserved today in Greccio. He is also most likely to have met those who had known Francis and his companions. And it is more than probable that he had read what Thomas of Celano, the Luke of Francis, had written about him. There is a remarkable likeness between the works of these two portraitists – one in paint, one in words – not only in the physical features, but in the spirit they have captured of the man.

Celano was probably only three years younger than Francis and was received into the Order by the Saint himself at the age of about thirty. He did not get to know Francis for long from close. But the little that he knew of him – the words he had heard from him with his own ears, the actions he had seen with his own eyes, the hours he had spent in his presence – these he treasured in his memory and pondered over and over. Later, in the prologue to his life of Saint Francis he was to write with some pride that he was recording "things I have heard from his own mouth", and with humility, "or what I have gathered from faithful and trustworthy witnesses". He must have gone around gathering every scrap of information he could from those who knew him better, and carefully jotted them down in his notebook.

In the days that followed the death of Francis the friars felt within them a gnawing void that it seemed nothing on earth would ever fill, and a wound that would take a long, long time to heal. As each night descended, this lostness and heaviness would take hold of them, the darkness would lie like a pall over them, and on every mind would be the same question, "Will it ever be dawn again?" Like children they would huddle together around the fire and talk of the voice that was silent and the place that lay empty at table and at choir. Telling the stories they remembered, they would often repeat themselves or each other, for they were not speaking to pass on information, they were clutching at a ritual to soothe their wound. I see Thomas in that group, with his eyes fixed on the burning logs and his heart drinking in every word. They lived in a less self-conscious age than ours, and cried often. I see Thomas wiping his tears as he stores everything away in his memory, while the night wears on. Thus with these hooded figures sitting around the flames night after night, their memories, like ghosts, would wander through the roads of Umbria, the Valley of Rieti, the rocky forests of Fonte Colombo, the peaks of La Verna and Narni and the rivulets of Celle de Cortona, and would come back with the wild flowers they had gathered and place them at the shrine of their master. And slowly, as the weeks and the months went by, there rose from the cinders the figure of Francis that Thomas etched for posterity – and benignly haunts my dreams today, and those of thousands like me.

Brother Thomas was the first to write them all down, and he wrote with such feeling that they are still warm today. He takes us in to join that group by the fire to watch the dance of the flames and to see there the man they so loved:

> O how beautiful he was, how splendid, how glorious
> in the innocence of his life,
> in the simplicity of his words,
> in the purity of his heart,
> in his love for God and his love for his brothers,
> in the promptness of his obedience,
> the gentleness of his bearing;
> how angelic was his countenance!
> He was charming in his manners, quiet in his ways,

gracious in his speech, prudent in his advice,
trustworthy in his duty, wise in his counsels,
efficient in his work and graceful in all things.

He was serene of mind,
sweet of disposition, sober of spirit;
in contemplation exalted, in prayer unwavering,
and in all things fervent.
He was constant in purpose, stable in virtue,
rooted in grace and in all things true to himself.
He was quick to pardon, slow to take offence,
ready of wit, retentive of memory,
sharp in discussions, careful in decisions,
and in all things simple.
Austere with himself, but gentle with others,
he was always discreet.
He was a most eloquent man,
his face always cheerful, his expression kindly.
There was no trace of cowardice in him,
yet he was never arrogant.

He was of medium height, more short than tall,
his head was of moderate size and round,
his face somewhat long and distinguished,
his forehead smooth and narrow,
his eyes were of normal size,
black, and lucid with sincerity.
His hair was black, his eyebrows straight,
his nose regular, delicate and slender;
his ears were upright, but small, his temples smooth.

His speech was peaceable, but fiery and pungent,
his voice powerful, but sweet, clear and musical.
His teeth were well set, even and white,
his lips were small and thin,
his beard dark and rather sparse,
his neck was slender, his shoulders straight,

his arms were short, his hands slight,
with long, tapering fingers and nails.
His legs were thin, his feet small.
He was lean and delicate-skinned,
and wore rough clothes.
He slept little, and gave things away bountifully.
In this great humility
he showed great kindness to everyone,
and adapted his manners to all kinds of people.
Though holier than the saints,
among sinners he was like one of them.

Out of this delicate mosaic lovingly pieced together from fragments brought by the collective memory of those who knew him, had lived with him – and missed him so badly – Francis walks up to me today with all his simplicity and goodness. With the holiness of his life he comes as a frightening challenge, but he puts me at ease, because "he adapted his manners to all kinds of people". All kinds of people – that is comforting!

New Mosaic

As a Franciscan I look at him and I see that each one who wants to know Francis and follow him must form his own mosaic of his face just as Thomas of Celano made his. Thomas met him; so must I. Thomas spoke with the men who knew him; so must I. Piece by piece I must collect stones of many colours from whoever can offer them and must fit them together, not with study only, but also with the affections of the heart. And of this portrait I should be able to say to Francis at the end of my life what Thomas did at the end of his book, "though it is not done as well as you deserve, it is done lovingly, to the best of our ability".

Pieces for this mosaic must be picked primarily from Francis' own writings, the authentic sources, and from scholarly studies made of these. It is important that we learn what history has recorded about Francis and his times. Every bit of information we can find about his background, the forces that went into the making of his character and the influence he had on his contemporaries must be gathered. In this matter, fortunately, ever newer pieces of evidence have been coming up and valuable studies are constantly being published. We can ignore these only at the peril of forming in our minds a Francis that may be very beautiful, but one that never existed.

But we should not be content with history. It would be good to keep in mind that history as a science in our sense of the term (of recording and reconstructing exactly what happened and as it happened) is little more than a hundred years old, having been devised and perfected by the German historian Von Ranke (1795–1886). We know that the Bible, even in its historical parts, was not written by "scientific historians", but by poets, seers and theologians, who knew that the truth they had to tell was truer than facts. So too were the Franciscan sources written not by "scientific historians", but by lovers of Francis, a fact we can hardly miss while reading through the texts.

Francis is one of those figures whom history is too narrow to contain. His song and laughter are too loud for its pages. We have to search the legends, look between the petals of the "Little Flowers", and the stories that have grown by the pathways in the countryside. Malcolm Muggeridge expressed a great truth when he said, "Legends seem to me more relevant to our human situation, and in that sense more 'factual' than history, which is really only the propaganda of the victor . . . If and when we know the final truth about human life, we shall find that the legends, or what pass for legends, are far nearer the truth than what passes for fact or science or history."[2]

19

It is a rare form of greatness that belongs to people around whom legends grow easily, and whose personalities keep eluding study and mastery. There is always something more to be said about them, because they are within us. They are the people who have the power to disturb and shake our depths, as well as the power to build us up and to bring out the best in us.

The lovers of Francis, who have allowed themselves to be shaken and built up in this way, are an army. Their tramping resounds through eight centuries and their ranks keep swelling still. Among this multitude are men and women of acute sensitivity and perception who have risen from the love of Francis to a personal experience of him, and have captured that experience in words, lines, paint, stone, wood, sound or film. Stumbling upon their works we too can be lifted to similar experiences.

Therefore another mine to dig for truly precious stones for the portrait is fiction. Felix Timmermans or Louis de Wohl or Murray Boldo[3] can take you on a pilgrimage where you are so lost in the glory of the landscape and the company of Francis that the milestones really do not matter. Eloi Leclerc, who has given us scholarly studies, has shown himself to be greater than a scholar by walking into the land of fiction and in *The Wisdom of the Poverello*, calling up a Francis of flesh and blood who eats with us and communes with us. *Francis of Assisi* by Nikos Kazantzakis is an arena where two great men, Nikos and Francis, have met and conversed and wrestled together in profound fellowship. To ask how authentic or historical these are is like asking how many pounds Tuesday weighs or what is the algebraic formula for moonlight on the seascape.

Poetry, art, drama, music, cinema and all other art forms too must be combed. Muggeridge said, "Only mystics, clowns and artists, in my experience, speak the truth, which, as

Blake was always insisting, imagination alone can grasp."[4]
Dante, Alfred Noyes, El Greco, Rembrandt, Franco Zeffirelli
and others have encountered Francis in their own private
gardens and have kept a seat for us to join in. We need not
agree with everything they say. The function of art and
fiction is not to give information about the historical Saint
Francis but to wake up the Francis that is within us and put
him in touch with the conscious part of us. Into such a
garden we have to enter with reverence and fantasy – and a
bit of humour – and we shall meet Francis, not merely learn
about him.

Such a search must never be a substitute for probing
history. It must take off from where history stops. Thus, for
instance, I would not recommend Kazantzakis' *Francis* to
someone who does not have a knowledge of the historical
Francis *and* does not know what to make of his type of
fiction. As in most forms of art, Kazantzakis distorts reality
(which should be kept in mind) in order to bring alive
another dimension of Francis. Once we accept this, we shall
find that he opens up the pores of our soul. We shall then
learn to make playful and prayerful use of our own fantasy,
and come to an entirely new and enriching sort of
understanding. "Understanding" may not be the word for
it; perhaps "seeing" is better. People who have not "seen"
in that way are likely to find it foolish.

One evening at San Damiano one of the Fathers told me he
was going to Gubbio the next morning and I could come
along if I cared to. I was delighted and told the novices
jokingly I was going to meet the wolf of Gubbio. They told
me the wolf of Gubbio did not exist, it was only a legend. I
said no, I was determined to meet him. We arrived at
Gubbio around ten and said mass at the shrine of the local
patron saint, whose feast it was. After lunch my friend told
me he had some work elsewhere and would meet me
around five. He dropped me off at the art museum and

21

suggested I could spend the afternoon there. Now, I do love spending time in art museums, but not in a place like Gubbio, that quaint little town on a hill that drips with the honey of the Francis legend. The legend tells of how he went out all alone to meet the fierce wolf that had been terrorizing the countryside and spoke to him and tamed him and brought him to the city to live the rest of his life as the pet of everyone.

When my friend drove off, I decided to do a bit of exploring for my wolf. I started walking and asked everyone I came across in my halting Italian if they could tell me where Saint Francis had tamed the wolf. Some told me politely they did not know, some looked at me as if I could do with some professional psychiatric help. Finally I saw a little girl skipping rope by the road and repeated the question that I knew by heart now. Her eyes brightened. Ah yes, she understood what I meant. I had only to go that way, turn left, then right and left again and walk a little more . . . "And a little child shall lead them." I followed her instructions and came upon the loveliest of old chapels and a marble slab which said "The Chapel of Brother Wolf". The chapel was locked, but the surrounding area was open ground, and there I was, all alone, with some four hours to myself. I found a tree stump that looked a little like a wolf looking into the sky. It looked like a dead tree but it wasn't dead, it was only waiting for a few more days of the spring sun to burst into life. I stood a long time there lost in the experience, and made a sketch of the scene, trying not to force the likeness of the wolf. The life within that tree that had slept all through the winter and was ready to wake up was now reaching out to the depths within me, and before I knew it, it was time to go back to the museum and meet my confrère. Now, don't tell me the wolf of Gubbio did not exist. I have met him; he is right within me. I was there when Brother Francis had a long talk with him and shall not easily forget it.

The chapel of
Brother Wolf in Gubbio

There is more to the wolf of Gubbio than a historic four-footed beast. We miss the whole story if we forget that we are all wolves to each other and what makes us so most of the time is fear. Fear builds up walls between people and between nations. Fear builds up stockpiles of nuclear weapons, in many senses. Francis broke down that fear and replaced it with trust when he went out alone and spoke to the wolf. He was doing the same thing in different ways all the time – when he embraced the leper, when he begged in the streets of Assisi, when he converted the robbers of Monte Casale, when he went out to meet the Sultan of Egypt, when he reconciled the mayor and the Bishop of Assisi. By trusting and making himself vulnerable he tamed the wolf – and does still. The wolf is real.

Looking for the Centre

Just as the gathering of "historical data" is only a part, though an important one, of this process, so too are the study and laborious practice of what are called "Franciscan virtues". Looking for the heart of the Franciscan vocation in virtues can be quite an unnerving thing. There was that Sister who once said to me, "I was taught in my noviciate that there are certain virtues and characteristics that are distinctly Franciscan, like love, joy, poverty, simplicity, humility, Christ-centredness, etc. In recent years I have been working with members of other religious groups and with lay people, and even with non-Catholics; and I have found these virtues among them as much as among Franciscans. These are in fact Christian virtues. So, why can't we say, let's be good Christians? Why be Franciscans at all?"

Now, that is a question one cannot answer, for there are no REASONS why anyone should be a Franciscan, just as there are no REASONS why anyone should be a Christian. There is much more to it all than reason.

But if the question be re-phrased thus: "Is it meaningful to be a Franciscan? Is there anything distinctive about

Franciscan life?" we shall find that the millions who have borne that name through eight centuries and still do, stand ready to give the answer, if only by their numbers.

In one sense the meaning and point of Franciscan life is as precise and distinctive as anything could be, and in another, just as mysterious and elusive.

The heart of the Franciscan vision for me is simply this man, Francesco Giovanni di Pietro Bernardone, as clear, distinct and unique as any man could be, who might be walking down the road. To be a Franciscan is to be enamoured of this person, just as Leo, Rufino, Angelo and others were in his time. They did not follow him because they wanted to imitate the virtues he practised, or because they found his ideas interesting; they followed him because he was Francis and they could not help wanting to be his friends.

The Shadows

A true friend is one who loves you because of what your are, and also in spite of what you are. The friends of Francis had to stand the test of this second part too, and will always have to.

For Francis had his peculiarities and his idiosyncrasies, some of them magnified for us and even made ridiculous with the passage of time and the change of cultures. Like the prophets he carried his dramatic gestures to extremes in order to live his convictions to the full or to drive home his points. When he washed his hands he would be careful not to set foot on "Sister Water" (I wonder how he washed his feet then?). When his habit caught fire he would not put it out, out of reverence for the Creator of "Brother Fire". Invited to lunch with a cardinal of the Church and sitting at table with important guests, he would take out his little begging bowl filled with stale soup, mouldy bread and discarded meat and vegetables that he had collected from door to door. He would not only proceed to eat out of it, but

25

pass it around to let everyone have the privilege of "partaking of the table of the Lord".

Francis was also inconsistent. He insists that the friars should own nothing, "neither a place nor a house nor anything" and then cheerfully goes and accepts the gift of a mountain. He writes that "if the friars are not wanted somewhere, they should go to another place to do penance with the blessing of God", and then tells them they should never leave the Portiuncula, and if they are "driven out by one door, should come in by another". In his Testament he says, "Let not the brethren say this is another rule; it is only a reminder, an admonition, an exhortation and my testament", and goes on to say at least five times, "I strictly command you by holy obedience".

You cannot leave these out in studying the Spirit at work in Francis. They were part of the man and, to me, they are what make him so unique and lovable. I think it was François Mauriac who called Jesus "the most quiveringly real of history's great figures and, out of all the human types it offers, the least logical, because the most alive."

I can imagine a lot of great people – a Benedict, a Thomas Aquinas, a Teresa of Avila, an Ignatius, an Einstein – as being perfectly logical and consistent people. But a perfectly logical Francis would be just a great man, and not Francis of Assisi.

I thank God for all the incongruencies of Francis' character, because by these the man I would like to idolize and worship becomes my fellow traveller and takes my hand in his.

This man, Francis, then, with all his lights and all his shadows, this man as he was and keeps on being in the hearts of his friends, this man is for me the point where Franciscan living finds its meaning. Nothing could be more definite or precise.

Search for the Charism

That leads to the question, how do you define him and his charism? That is a question that has bothered a great many people in the past, and let us hope will bother a great many in the future.

In a religious founder we can distinguish three elements: 1. his (or her, of course) personal character; 2. his cultural environment; and 3. the special charism given him by the Spirit of God. Of these his followers commit themselves only to the third. They are not to re-live his personal life, nor re-create his cultural milieu. Their vow is to re-live, in their own personal character and cultural background of place and time, the charism of the founder.

But this charism is not something that can be supplied ready-made as a formula to be followed. Such formulae and studies may be in existence, but still the charism has to be discovered again by each individual and community in a dynamic, creative and on-going process. In that process, constant reference to the person of the founder in the context of his or her culture and times can be of value. In the case of some saints this can be of greater value – with some, indispensable.

There are saints whose work and ideals reflect the holiness of the Church and the greatness of God so brilliantly that their personalities hide behind these. There are others whose very personalities capture and reflect the Church's holiness and God's goodness in an outstanding way, and their works and the inspiration they leave behind only shine with that brilliance. Saint Francis is undoubtedly the most outstanding example of the latter.

Eric Doyle O.F.M. in his book *Francis and the Song of Brotherhood* makes an interesting remark in this connection. Talking about the Rule of Saint Francis, he says, "As a

Rule it is intimately bound up with Francis' insight into what it means to be loved by God in Christ and with his daily experience of love. It is inseparable from the man himself. I do not think the Benedictines would say that their Rule is inseparable from St Benedict. It seems to me that even if St Benedict had never existed, the Rule would still stand in its own right and command respect, devotion, loyalty and love. This is not the case with the Rule of St Francis. Without him the Rule is all but unintelligible. And this, I submit, is what makes it unique among Rules in the Western Church."[5]

Another great founder so interestingly different from Francis is his own contemporary and friend, St Dominic Guzman. Dominic responded to the needs of his times (and of all times), and re-activated preaching in the Church as a basic pattern of Christian living so powerfully that when he died his confrères were more interested in continuing his work than in writing about his personal life and holiness. The earliest account we have of Dominic is not called *A life of St Dominic*, but *A Little Book about the Beginnings of the Order of Preachers*.[6]

But already in the lifetime of Francis there were so many stories about him going around (the kind of stories that anyone would *love* to tell), that on the very day of his funeral the Pope commissioned the writing of his biography. And it took Celano two years to finish, for he had an enormous amount of material at his disposal. Today an *Omnibus* of only the important sources fills nearly 2,000 pages.

Dominic claimed no special place in his brotherhood, and always insisted on being treated as "one of the brothers". Interestingly, Saint Francis seldom uses that term about himself. When he speaks about himself in relation to the brothers, he is usually either "the least of the brothers and their servant" or their "father" and their "model". Francis was nothing if not dramatic. And he had that particular way of being dramatic, which disarmed and captivated. The memory of such a man haunts.

That charm of Francis' personality, which always intrigued and fascinated, and still does, is what I consider to be an integral part of his charism, which otherwise would make no sense.

That brings us back to the question of how to understand his personality. It is here that the answers begin to be elusive. Here begins the mystery – and the adventure. We can always begin to answer the question, as thousands have done before, but we shall never have finished with it. The reason, very simply, is that Francis is a person, and that Francis is Francis.

People

It can never be said too often that the person of Christ is the soul of Christianity, not his teachings, ideas or approach to life; they are part of it, but not its soul. To understand Jesus – not with the brains only, but with the heart and the whole soul – and to grow into him, we need the help of other persons – our parents, teachers, neighbours, friends and the ministers of the Church. God comes to us, and we go to God, through human relationships. Theology can help, but it is people who mediate.

In the ancient *Gurukul* system of education in India the *Guru* was not merely a schoolmaster whose classes you attended. You had to live in his house and offer your unquestioning submission to his authority. Only then could he lead you into the art of living and the knowledge of God.

The history of Christianity is dotted with charismatic figures of varying greatnesses who have been given to Christians in order to lead them to God. Together with them they form the Body of Christ, where each part is related to the other, and only thus to the Head. In our search for God intermediaries are not an obstacle, they are even necessary.

Christ and Francis

I have never in all my life seen my fascination for Francis to be in conflict with that for Christ. Both pull me with an immense force. Though there is an infinity between the planes on which they pull, it is like one gravity. The attraction of Francis makes sense only in relation to that of Jesus.

Francis is for me the life-giving principle of the Franciscan way of life. But not in the sense that Jesus is the life-giving principle of the Church. If Jesus is the Way, our one and only way to the Father, Francis is not a lane beside or a way within the Way, but our fellow-traveller, a fellow-traveller who lightens the trek because he sings along the way, though not without tears.

If Jesus is the Truth and the Life, Francis is not an abridged edition of the truth or some substitute vital force, but a humble and earnest seeker.

If Jesus is the Master, our one and only Master, Francis is not another master or a tutor, but a fellow-disciple with us, the keenest in the group. His eyes, as I see him, have that sparkle which keeps telling us that learning at the feet of this Master is indeed a joyous affair.

Christ, the person of Jesus Christ, is our only way to God; he is both the way and the end of the way, both the search and the treasure. On this way God has given me a fascinating guide in the person of Francis of Assisi. He too is one who challenges me with force, but his is not another or a new challenge. Having gone through the mill along with Jesus, the mill of suffering-to-glory, death-to-life, bitter-to-sweet, he interprets Jesus' challenge for me with a freshness and a vitality that happen to grip me as no other interpretation does.

That I have been brought under the charm of this vision and this man is a grace and a mystery that to this day continues to baffle me. And being caught in this vision I do not think any other vision of the Gospel would be valid for me. In itself the religious vocation and the Gospel vision of one particular religious founder is no better than that of any other. But for each individual the vision God has called him to share is not only better than all others, but the only one good enough.

Not merely to be Christian

The Franciscan vision is not simply the Christian vision, and Francis wanted his followers to be not merely good Christians. A reading of the sources cannot miss the fact that Francis himself saw his own grasp of the Gospel as revealed to him by God and as being distinct from any other. At the Chapter of Mats an attempt was made to persuade him to change his way of life in the light of other religious orders. His answer was, "In truth God has revealed this way for me and for all who are willing to trust and follow me. So I do not want you to quote any other rule to me, whether that of St Benedict, St Augustine or St Bernard, or any other form of life except this way which the Lord in his mercy has shown and given to me. The Lord has called me to be a new kind of fool in this world, and he does not want us to live by any other wisdom but this."[7] Benedict, Augustine and Bernard were good enough Christians and Francis had no quarrel with their rules. But his was simply a different way of life; the Lord wanted him and his followers to live by that, and no other.

There were plenty of things Francis considered to be perfectly legitimate for all Christians, but not for himself and his followers – such as holding positions of authority, riding on horseback, owning property or using money. He expressedly told his brothers to wear cheap and coarse garments themselves, but not to despise or look down upon

31

people who wore stylish and expensive clothes. He wanted his followers to be not merely Christians, but Christians in a particular manner, the manner the Lord had revealed to him.

Part of this particular manner was a certain inter-relationship among those who shared this vision. They had to be "brothers", not only to all people, but very specially among themselves, and there had to be a community of those who saw the world in that particular way. And Francis unmistakably saw himself, as the early brothers saw him, as the model for the other brothers, and as their leader and father. Under God he was the fountain-head of the vision, and thus part of it.

Franciscan life is therefore a life-long search into the personality, and thus the charism, of Saint Francis of Assisi in the only way he would want to be studied – as a disciple of Jesus.

Adventure

Searching into a personality is a most adventurous thing; every day we shall be discovering new depths and we shall never reach the end of the search. I once saw this beautifully expressed in a film. The man and the woman were walking towards each other from the right and the left of the frame. But they were on two separate shots super-imposed. Each of them kept walking towards the other, but they never met. It is a search that is endless, and we shall never be able to capture or master the object of our search. The meaning of the search lies in the search itself, and the continual discovery of new depths. It is a plunge into an infinity – the reason why religious life, as well as marriage, can be nothing less than a commitment until death.

Basic to this approach to the Franciscan vocation is the assumption that the charism of Saint Francis is a living, growing, reality. Essentially it is not something that can be found in books, though books are helpful, even indispensable. The living organism where we discover this charism is in the first place the community of Brothers or Sisters to which we have been called, and in the second place the community which is the larger Franciscan family.

United in a bond of brotherly love and mutual acceptance they share their insights and experience in living out this charism. In the light of the Gospel and in prayer they constantly study the sources of Franciscanism – the Rule, the writings and the life of Francis – and their own constitutions in the light of these. The life and writings of the early followers of Francis and the way they shared his charism are also studied, as well as the way it has been understood, explained and lived by Franciscans through the centuries down to our own day. From such a prayerful study and lived sharing, in the context of modern situations and problems, there arises a rapport with the person of Francis and an understanding of his charism that are endlessly on-going and fulfilling.

I find this endless discovery most fascinating. I happen to be writing this in our house of noviciate in Palmaner (from notes made in Assisi). When I was a novice here we went out of the enclosure once in a while, when our novice-master thought a little walk would do good to our calves (and to our souls). The rest of the time we spent within the walls, praying, studying, working, together. The canonical enclosure was strictly observed too. Outsiders, especially women, were never allowed in. I learnt a great deal about Saint Francis that year. But the novices of today, over thirty years later, have a slightly different life-style. Every week they spend half a day out in the woods or fields having their "desert experience" of prayer. Another half day is spent at the local leprosy hospital. Sometimes they spend a whole day out, building huts for the poor leprosy patients in the locality. Our guests are brought inside the friary often, and they eat with us. What has happend during these years is that the door of the Franciscan friary has received a new definition; "coming in" and "going out" have begun to take on new meanings, less monastic and more in keeping with the mind of Francis and our times. This has been possible because friars, open to the stirrings of new winds in the Church and the Order, and to new insights into Francis, have studied and reflected together, and have dared to make changes. By this I come to understand more of Francis.

Visiting Franciscan Brothers and Sisters of different congregations in different places I have received the most unexpected flashes of insight into the charismatic personality of Francis. There are always new and the most undreamt-of discoveries waiting for us, sometimes in the most unlikely of corners. A chance remark of a Brother, or a twitch on the face or an inflection in the voice of a Sister, revealing a hidden sacrifice or an unexpected warmth of kindness, tells us that Francis of Assisi is very much alive today.

I find it an absorbingly interesting thing to be a Franciscan, as long as there is a man like Francis around, to keep coaxing the best in people to come out. As on a vast seashore, every day I pick up new pebbles of many colours for my mosaic. And the portrait keeps growing. New wrinkles, new shades, fresh nuances of character keep on appearing.

Words fail when you want to say thank you to the Lord for a man like this. That is why I would like to borrow a few lines from the Canticle of Brother Sun (with due apologies to its author):

Most high, almighty, gracious Lord,
yours is all praise and honour and glory and blessing.

PRAISE BE TO YOU, MY LORD, FOR BROTHER FRANCIS

To you alone do they belong, Most High,
and no man is worthy to utter your name.
Praise be to you, my Lord, for all your creatures,
chiefest of all for Sir Brother Francis!
He is our day, through him you give us light.
Beautiful is he, and radiant, and bright in splendour,
he lights up for us our path to you.

2 Child of the Landscape

WE ALL HAVE a private collection of memories of beauty – scenes, faces, works of art, fantasies, dreams, which have pierced us through with their sheer loveliness and put us in touch with another world. Occasionally they come back, sometimes in fragments, in our dreams or when we relax on a tired day.

Prominent in my collection is a view of Assisi on the eve of the feast of Saint Francis in 1971. After supper a friar at Chiesa Nuova, where I was staying then, said, "Let's go for a ride to see the city illuminated." Assisi is built on the slope of a mountain, with a larger mountain, Subasio, standing behind it. We drove out of the city towards the Portiuncula in the plains, and stopped halfway, at the precise spot where Saint Francis on his last journey before death had asked the friars to stop and lay his stretcher down with his face to the city, and blessed it. We do not know what it was that Francis saw at that time. Probably it was a view of his city more glorious and heavenly than anyone had ever seen or will ever see, for he was blind then.

Assisi

But I know what I saw. I have only to close my eyes to see it all over again. The castle on top of the hill and the churches and important buildings were floodlit. All the buildings were dotted with tiny lights, not electric lights but live flames from oil lamps that twinkled and shimmered in the distance. Above the city hung an unusually large full moon that had just risen from behind Subasio and wore a light orange colour to match the flames below. And covering it all like a large block of some rare, transparent, precious stone in which the city was embedded as a result of some primeval volcanic eruption, was a gentle mist that had descended from heaven for the occasion.

We must have stood there a long time. Or was it five minutes? I do not know. I did not have my camera with me, and in a way I am glad, for then I would have cut out a neat rectangular piece from the centre of what my eyes were seeing and fixed it on paper or film, and not retained in memory the scene in its entirety, the atmosphere and the sheer experience of being a participant in that "event" which was enveloping us.

Near to where we stood was a bronze plaque depicting the scene of Francis blessing his city from his deathbed. Beneath it a marble slab carried the text of the blessing. But we did not have to read that text. We were seeing it before us, not with our eyes only, but with our whole being. From words that blessing had been transformed into that mist which covered us, the city, the mountain, the moon and the whole sky.

The Blessing

The last blessing of Francis still rests over Assisi. It is there for anyone to see, though pilgrims see it more clearly than tourists do.

And it rests on whatever Francis has touched in Italy, the many sanctuaries that dot Umbria and its neighbourhood, the mountain tops, the caves, the rock-fastnesses, the hermitages, the valleys, the roads. All these are places where he had experiences of God so strong and so scorching they had to leave some warmth for future travellers.

Pilgrims from the time of Saint Francis to our own have testified to this in the most glowing and eloquent terms. Their list includes Dante, Jacopone da Todi, Giovanni Papini, Emile Ripert, Alfred Noyes, Gabriel Fauré, Evelyn Underhill, Clare Sheridan, Louis de Cardonell, Pope John XXIII and Pope John Paul II. Even today people who go to Assisi come away with a feeling quite unique, of having set foot on the arena of some overwhelming God-experience.

I had been reading and studying about Saint Francis for years and I thought I knew him – till I went to Assisi. My most startling discovery there was that I had never really known him till then. Or known him in that particular way. Those quaint stories about him, the odd and funny things he did, those delightful inconsistencies and idiosyncrasies of his, the unbelievably harsh manner in which he treated his body, the great tenderness he had for other people and for all things living, the love of God which was a bonfire within him – all these things suddenly become credible in that place, not credible in an intellectual sort of way, but in a way far more compelling and far less yielding to scrutiny and analysis. There you find yourself saying, "Now I can see why he was like that; now I can believe Celano and Bonaventure and all the rest – even the *Fioretti*."

More than any other saint or great personage, Saint Francis lingers on in the places where he was born and lived, because more than anyone else he allowed himself to be shaped by them. It was most fitting indeed that the conclusion and climax of his "Canticle of Brother Sun", as he originally conceived it, should be about "our sister, Mother Earth, who sustains us and feeds us and governs us." The earth with its mountains and valleys, its trees, flowers and fruits nourished his soul and shaped him, and received from him the gift of a rare eloquence.

Trees

The trees of Umbria speak his language. They lead you to the heart of all trees and teach you to commune with them.

There is something about the way trees grow that seems to reach out to our deepest roots. Why are trees so interesting? Why have people of all countries and all civilizations found them so mysterious? The ancient Greeks, Aztecs, Norsemen and Swedes, Semites, Aryans, Druids, have all surrounded their trees with stars and angels and divine voices. Moses saw God in a tree; Adam and all his progeny found in it their death – and their life.

I began to understand trees when I came across this sentence somewhere: "God is the sum of all the possibilities." A tree is always searching for and moving out to new ways of being. A tree has initiative, imagination and hope. Though it knows its laws, there is always a touch of the unpredictable about it. Yet its inventiveness is seasoned with wisdom – "change the things I can, accept the things I cannot". Every shadow that falls on it and every wind that blows gives it shape. Trees thus establish communion with our own fantasy, our ingenuity, our hope, our resignation.

It is no wonder that Francis was especially tender towards trees and all things growing. He found in them altars where in the most extraordinary and poetic ways he could bring his worship to the One who is "the sum of all the possibilities".

When brothers went out to the forest to cut wood, he would tell them not to cut down the entire tree, but to leave a stump behind so that it might have hope of sprouting again. How the man understood trees! Can anything on earth speak more loudly or more clearly of hope and all the possibilities that hide in hope and all the explosive power of hope than a tree stump?

And in his garden he liked a little disorder. He used to tell the brother gardener to keep a part of it untilled so that the grass and wild flowers might come up on their own and talk to us of God.

There are two ways of making and tending a garden. You can make all the paths straight and the flower-beds in perfect geometrical order and keep the hedges neatly trimmed. This is very efficient, very logical and very exact. Everything according to plan. It gives you a sense of mastery; you can see what is where.

Or you can make the paths twist and turn, the way a tree grows, and you can allow the bushes and trees to be themselves a little more. You walk in such a garden not because you want to get from one place to another most efficiently, but because walking is good. And as you turn and turn again, you come upon things you did not see at the beginning. It leads you to expect the unforeseen, leaves room for mystery. It is a little like a fairy-tale garden where miracles can spring on you any time. The trees invite you to sit under them and to contemplate.

Such a garden stands for a totally different outlook on life. A twisting and rambling path shows a concept of time and an approach to the mysteries of life which do not quite tally with the positivistic, achievement-centred, success-minded ways of modern Western civilization.

The broad, straight and long gravel path with its neatly laid and painted borders of brick, and its hedges in perfect line tells you: "You are in control; to every question you can find an answer." But the path that goes over the bridge, twists under the tree and reveals a new wild flower by the rock slows you down and says:

> The angels keep their ancient places;
> Turn but a stone and start a wing:
> 'Tis ye, 'tis your estranged faces
> That miss the many-splendoured thing.
> (*Francis Thompson*)

Assisi (and the whole of Franciscan Italy) is one such garden of fairyland where you have to take off your shoes. Don't go there if you do not have time and are not prepared to become a child again and make yourself a bit of a fool. An entire scale of values has to be set aside as you pass the gate. Everything stops you to tell you secrets, and you will miss all the secrets if you have to rush because the bus is waiting.

There is a subtle and rare gift the place and the man it enshrines offer to those willing to take it, the gift of seeing and hearing and wondering, and the gift of s-l-o-w-i-n-g d-o-w-n to LIVE.

The City

The city of Assisi is not a city, but a town so small you can walk from one end of it to the other in about twenty minutes. Perched on the instep of Mount Subasio, it has been called "the most harmoniously built city in the world". It was not designed. Without a plan it just grew, following a pattern etched in the minds of thousands of Umbrian builders through the centuries, the way a beehive grows, following the pattern etched in the brains of hundreds of bees. To your right as you approach the city from the railway station of Santa Maria Degli Angeli is the green-blue-grey Mount Subasio in the distance. The line of the mountain runs down to the left and then rises a little to show up the medieval fortress, Rocca Maggiore. There Francis at the age of sixteen probably took part in its siege and demolition by the citizens of Assisi when the hated Duke Conrad of Lutzenfeld was away. He may also have taken part in the building of the city walls with its stones, at least at some of the lighter jobs, and enjoyed the work and made it enjoyable for the others. From the Rocca the line continues and meets that other castle, the Basilica of Saint Francis, where the body of the saint rests today, a castle of the spirit. In a horizontal line to the right of the basilica sprawls the city with its church towers and domes, its houses and walls built of that peculiar flesh-coloured stone of Subasio which throbs with life in the sun.

There is a kind of playful mischief about the streets of Assisi, twisting and turning, rising and falling suddenly, sitting still and then jumping up, like kittens frolicking. They are likely to come up with the most unexpected twists of fancy. A road is quietly ambling along, and then suddenly decides to turn left and then changes its mind and turns back to orthodoxy and goes on, sometimes for the obvious reason that it was searching for a better view over the valley, or sometimes for no reason at all. Why do children run and jump when they can walk, and why do they swing and zigzag when they can go straight?

The houses enjoy springing surprises on you; they are not coldly rigid and logical. They reveal unexpected nooks and corners where people can relate and share secrets. They are not static things, but things with a life of their own, that have forgotten to stop growing. They have stories to tell, and their walls are pasted over with memories – a window here that once was a door; an arch there that once opened to the northern skies but later consented to be walled up in favour of a window looking eastward to the rising sun; a one-time cupboard which like a chrysalis has burst out into a window and is perched there ready to fly away. Those houses recall Gibran's words, "Your house is your larger body. It grows in the sun and sleeps in the stillness of the night; and it is not dreamless. Does not your house dream? and dreaming, leave the city for grove or hilltop?"

The streets call themselves by the most imaginative of names, unlike their counterparts in the big modern cities that prefer the highly efficient alternative of numbers. You will stumble upon the "Street of Pope Gregory the Great" and find it is a narrow alley about fifty yards long. But there is colour there, and history. I would rather any time live on an alley named after Gregory the Great or Dante or Giotto than on the mathematically precise fifth and forty-first.

Their walls like jugglers display iron rings of varying sizes, larger ones for pots of geranium and smaller ones waiting to carry live torches when the city lights up for the feasts. Around arched doorways of houses climb roses with large flowers cascading down in a display of royal largesse or vines with the movements of ballet.

The centre of the city and of its social life now as then is the Piazza del Commune, the Town Square, overlooked by the

Roman Temple of Minerva, now a church of Our Lady. This temple was already two hundred years old when Jesus lived, and its Corinthian columns watched the preaching of St Brizio and St Crispoldo and the martyrdom of St Rutino in the third century A.D., the attacks by the Ostragoths, the Byzantines and the Longobards in the sixth century, the sacking of the city and the massacre of its people by Charlemagne in the eighth century, and the establishment of the communes in the eleventh. Under its shadow too the Troubadours and Jongleurs from Provence sang the glories of King Arthur and his Knights of the Round Table in the century that followed, while, absorbing it all and being shaped by the stories, the drama and the entire civilization of knighthood and chivalry, stood a wide-eyed, open-mouthed little boy in the crowd, named Francesco Bernardone.

The Mountain

If you walk from there to the north-eastern gate of the city, Porta Perlici, you can see the landscape behind Assisi, which is in clean contrast to the peaceful and fertile Valley of Spoleto in front. The loveliness here is of another kind, steep ravines, rugged paths and rocky mountainside. To your right rises Mount Subasio, nestling in one of its folds the hermitage of Carceri. *Carceri* means prisons. You can see why it is called that when you climb up there, about an hour's brisk walk. Buried in the forests of ancient trees which writhe and twist as if in agony are rocky caves, where Francis and his early companions used to retire to do their wrestling with God.

You can climb higher still to the peak of Mount Subasio and what awaits you is a peace that is as all-pervading as is the view. It was on a day in May that I went up there. Down in the plain that morning you would have thought it was going to be a cloudy, even rainy, day. But up there the sky was bluer than any I had seen, and heaven somehow seemed closer. There were no trees there, but only grass, of a deep, unusual kind of green, and sprinkled over it a bonanza of wild flowers, putting Solomon to shame in all his glory. I was with two men, one seventy years old and the other approaching seventy. Suddenly all three of us were children and ran around picking flowers. And above us danced and sang the larks of Umbria celebrating their freedom from sowing and reaping and gathering into barns.

The Man

It was an accumulation of all this that moulded the personality of Francis. That peculiar indigo which goes into the making of the Umbrian skies. The effervescence of the pinkish stone of Subasio from which the city seems to have been carved out by frolicsome elves and which carries in its veins the city's long history of wars and treaties and the common man's struggle for freedom. The torches and heraldic banners that still flutter during Assisi's festivities. The sublimity and peace of the heights of Subasio and of the many hermitages, with the unmatched La Verna towering above all of them into the clouds of heaven. The thick forests with gnarled trees clinging tenaciously to the rocks. The fissures and ravines that frighten you and at the same time call you to pray. The olives and the cypresses which have entirely different ways of saying "Peace!" The sounds of the bells, of winds in the trees, of fresh water cascading down in streams and rivulets. The music of the birds which fills the air from before dawn till after dusk, with the crickets and cicadas taking over at night, and all these sounds only deepening the silence and attuning your ears to the whisper of God. The taste of the sunshine, the winds, the rainfall and the earth that linger in the wine and the bread. The taste in your mouth of fresh parsley picked from the earth. And not least the smell of the earth itself and of the grass growing and of the wild flowers. It was all these that shaped Francis and gave him his character. Now they wear with pride the shape and character they received from him.

Coming away from Assisi is like waking from a dream in which you met Francis, shook hands with him, walked and spoke with him and ate with him. Pilgrims there invariably say you expect to meet him walking down the road any time. There are moments when I am not quite sure if I did or did not actually run into him on some of those cobbled streets and beaten tracks, a smallish man with a meagre something on his face for a beard, wearing a coarse grey habit with many patches, that reached down to several inches above his ankles, with unshod feet and quick, small steps, all lightness and grace. I don't know why he always walked to a side of the road even when it was a narrow lane. Perhaps it was his courtesy and the expectation that someone more important might be coming down the road any moment. In fact he could not think of anyone on earth who was not just that. His dark, keen eyes seemed to take in everything around. One moment he would be greeting a sparrow on a branch, the next he would be doing a quick side-step, because there was a wild flower in his path which he must not hurt, or a worm waiting to be picked up gently and placed in a less dangerous spot. He seemed to be always on the move, though he stopped often. To dash off from a hermitage somewhere high up on the mountains of Narni or Fonte Colombo, or La Verna (which took me some hours by bus and train to reach) and to rush back to a village miles away – all on foot – was child's play with him. The roads and pathways of Umbria, which, seen from any of the mountain tops, are like strings of spaghetti strewn over the green landscape, running up the hills and down the valleys, cutting through olive groves and bridging streams, then pirouetting, crossing each other and gliding off again, appear to be as much a part of his character as the lines on his face. He is part of it all. And as he walks along, there is something in his stride that seems to indicate that he has a long, long way yet to go and he has hardly begun, but when he sees you, he stops – and has plenty of time for you.

3 The Most Italian

A NORWEGIAN friend of mine went to the post office in Assisi one afternoon. The door was open, but there was no one behind the counters. He looked around a bit and saw somewhere a door slightly ajar. Noises were coming from behind it, so he knocked. After a long time a man came out and said they were not working today. My friend asked if it was a holiday or something. "No", he said, "officially it is a working day, but we are having a little birthday celebration inside", – and with a wink and a smile – "so we are not working". With some coaxing however he agreed to sell him some stamps.

You can react to a situation like this in two ways: with annoyance and indignation, or with amusement and pleasure. My friend's reaction was the latter, and included even some appreciation. He said to me with a hearty laugh, "Only in Italy can such things happen." I don't know if this is true, but if it is, I am glad there is such a place.

In the post offices, shops, market-places and streets of Italy and of Assisi I caught glimpses that led on to interesting discoveries. Certain aspects of the Italian character – at least of those I came to know – made me place question marks against things I had taken for granted, and helped me to understand the man I had come looking for, Francis of Assisi.

Crazy things can happen in Italy, as a result of which speed and efficiency are compromised. In this I must say Italy reminded me of my own country. Coming to Italy after having spent nearly two years in other parts of Europe and in America, one of the first things that came to my mind was: here I feel at home.

In India too we have inefficiency, plenty of it. I used to find this maddening. But after America, where speed and efficiency were Moloch, it began to take on new shades. There in Assisi, where the breath of Francis still lingers, I slowly found myself asking: after all, why on God's earth should everything be so terribly efficient? Would it really be catastrophic if we slowed down our pace a bit, and paused awhile occasionally and tried to catch up a little on the forgotten art of living?

I think the Italians have not forgotten it, at least not yet, by and large. They can still sit down with a *quartino* of wine and a good deal of laughter and forget there is work to be done. Of course, this is not as it should be, but I do think it is better than the other extreme where you sit down to work and forget there are such things as wine and laughter.

Pursuit of Happiness

Western civilization (which is not Western any more but is fast becoming a world civilization) is based on the principle that happiness in life depends on how much you can earn, and how much comfort and prestige you can buy with it, and how efficiently you can make all matter and all energy serve you. The important things in life are to work hard, earn money (the more of it the better), buy things, make a name for yourself, get to the top, make everything work for you, tackle problems in the most direct, efficient way, and in everything, get on! It is a whole attitude toward matter and the world, where respect, reverence, wonder and other human values are blunted by an exaggerated and one-sided view of God's original command to man to "master the earth". The bankruptcy of this approach to the world and the emptiness of its promises have already been shown up by the tiredness and ennui it has generated, and the social drop-outs of different shades it has brought about in our own times.

The ideals of the world in Saint Francis' times were basically no different from those of ours. And he made a conscious choice to drop out of that society and walk out on its values.

It cannot be said that all Italians are like that, but during my stay in Rome and in Assisi at different times, the ones I came across gave me the strong impression that a certain sense of humour, or sense of proportion, has kept them from buying wholesale the value system of the Western world. Their ideas of efficiency and the way they approach problems are different from what you find in other countries of the West, and I cannot quite shake off the feeling that theirs might be the saner way.

I remember a traffic jam in the *Piazza del Popolo* in Rome. I was walking along the footpath when my attention was caught, first by the sound. There must have been a few scores of those little Fiats there and in every single one of them was sitting an angry Italian (if you have not seen an angry Italian, you have not seen one of God's most delightful creations!), cursing like mad, gesticulating with one hand and tooting the horn with the other. It sounded like something out of Verdi or Wagner. I tried to imagine how an American public would handle such a situation. There would be no empty gesticulations, no tooting of horns, because they know these things do not help. They might curse, but with moderation, then they would go home, sit down and write letters to their senator and to three daily papers. Then there would be resolutions introduced and passed, and within a few months there would be one fly-over built this way and one that way; and the problem would be solved once and for all, efficiently. In the meantime a lot of Italians would prefer to tackle their traffic problems by cursing, making faces and tooting horns. This sort of thing does not achieve anything, of course, but it is my contention that when it comes to tackling your anger, frustration or aggresiveness, there is nothing in the wide world so therapeutic as sitting in your car and tooting that horn. I stood there and watched this *Sinfonia del Popolo* under the baton of the traffic police with some amusement. After a while the traffic cleared and all those Italians were on their way again, perfectly cool and composed, and whistling away.

Some of those people might have been late to work that day, but I doubt if any of them got stomach ulcers worrying about what effect it would have on the national economy.

The Price

Some idea of the high price modern technology is paying for efficiency can perhaps be had from the atmosphere that prevails in most of the Western world on a Friday afternoon. People are frantic and you would think there was an earthquake announced but for the broad smiles and the greeting everywhere, "Have a nice weekend". The whole week is geared to one thing: work hard, achieve, make money, do better than your neighbour. By Friday afternoon it becomes a compulsion to get away from it all and to breathe some country air and *live* for two days.

There is that interesting fallacy of labour-saving. You take the family out to dinner to save you the trouble of cooking. But to be able to pay for this, for denying yourself the satisfaction of buying the food, cooking it, watching it change its form, smell and taste, giving it a new identity and life-giving purpose and serving it up before the family, you have to go out and work eight hours a day, pushing a button or pulling a lever without the contentment of having *made* something for someone.

In most places if you want to cut a hedge in your garden, you go out and cut it. When it is finished you stand back and look at your handiwork; it is a little crooked here and just a bit wonky there, but it is your work. Then you sit down to a meal with a good appetite and go to bed and sleep the sleep of the tired. In some advanced countries they have a machine to do the job for them. They sit inside the thing and drive it by the hedge creating a racket like a dentist burrowing inside your mouth. They finish the job in half an hour and tell themselves what a lot of labour and time they saved, and then run around the block to get exercise! Or they go to one of those health spas where they can run on an electrified treadmill – perhaps a comic symbol of the culture, something on which you can run all day without going anywhere.

The tragedy of it all is that once you get caught in this treadmill, it is so hard to get out. The whole culture and economy are geared to close all escapes to a more human existence. The style and cost of living are such that if you want to live at all you must work to bolster the culture machine.

The Idol

Efficiency, profit, competitiveness and other ideals of the Western work-ethic do have a positive value in the Christian outlook, but when they pass a certain point in importance and go outside of a certain perspective, this value becomes negative.

As the prince of God's creation it is man's prerogative to have ideals, and to conquer the earth and subdue it is as glorious an ideal as there could be. But the moment you take an ideal too seriously and give it an ultimate value, it becomes a monster.

Instead of mastering the earth and bringing it to the service of his Creator, man has made his mastering of the earth itself into an idol.

It is thus that the total value of goods produced and services provided annually, called the Gross National Product, becomes the ultimate criterion in judging the excellence of a nation and its progress.

When the people of any country, be it Italy or any other, show a more or less general tendency not to bow to the G.N.P. idol because they find something else – like the joy of living – more worthwhile, it deserves the special notice of anyone interested in the message of Saint Francis.

Balance

The Italians may fail in taking their ideals of efficiency seriously enough, but they certainly cannot be accused of a general tendency to take them too seriously. I consider this to be a rare and special type of humour that enables them to accept and to live with the discrepancies between the ideal and the real.

This tension between the ideal and the real is reflected in the tension between law and life, a tension that is played out daily on the streets of Rome. Roman traffic is a delightful comedy to watch, enough to convince you that Italians must be geniuses at traffic sense, because they systematically break all the rules and still so many of them are alive. I once saw a man in a car crossing a red light in a busy intersection. The police flagged him down. He stopped the car right in the middle, got out, let off a shower of Italian words, got back in, banged the door and drove off. I could not follow what he said, but it certainly was not Hail Marys. The policeman merely shrugged his shoulders helplessly as if to say Amen, and went on with his job.

It would seem that the Italians have a sixth sense that tells them when to make exceptions to the law. For them the law is always something that has to be seen in the context of life-situations. It would be wrong to say they do not care for the law (though one does come across this often enough, like anywhere else). They are geniuses at formulating it and in fact do take it seriously, but not with the kind of ultimate seriousness that the Germans and Anglo-Saxons seem to give it.

It has been pointed out that this difference of temperament is at the root of some of the tension within the Catholic Church. The Romans make the law and it does not bother them too much if it is not applicable to every single situation in life; after all, it is only a law! But the Northern temperament wants the law to be something that can be observed in every single case. So the Saxons would want the law to be lenient and its observance strict, while the Italians would want the law to be strict and its observance lenient. The former is certainly more efficient, but the latter shows a better sense of humour, the ability to cope with a discrepancy, without lowering the ideals.

Francis

Francis of Assisi, who has been called "the most Italian of the saints and the most saintly of the Italians" stands here with a few small words for our civilization that lies trapped in its own ideals. The solution is not to run away from technology. That is not possible any more, except perhaps for small groups, if at all. The solution must be sought in the direction of fixing our bearings once again. Our values may have to be reshuffled.

Francis went farther than any Italian, or indeed anyone, in taking his dreams and his ideals seriously, but his genius lay in that he stayed just this side of too seriously.

As a young man his ideals were those of his father, the textile merchant. We have evidence that he was a successful salesman; people loved dealing with him. But he could do things that were very foolish from a business point of view. Like leaving the shop just like that and running after a beggar whom he had turned away in a moment of absentmindedness.

Later, knighthood and glory became his ideals. His military foray to Perugia having failed, he took up the challenge of Apulia and ordered the most expensive knightly armour available. All dressed up and mounted he was about to start when he saw a knight too poor to afford good armour and gave it away to him.

Perhaps his father bought him another suit. He set out with great bravado and the boast that he was coming back a knight. But after a day's journey he returned home a deserter, because he had a dream and heard voices!

Then after his conversion, poverty becomes his life's ideal, and more than an ideal, his "bride". He lives in utmost destitution and wants everything around the friars' dwellings to reflect this uncompromising poverty. But he makes one exception – the holy Eucharist must be reserved "*in locis pretiosis*", in places that are richly ornamented. Things that have to do with the liturgy and the divine office get pre-eminence. But here again he can make strange exceptions: once a poor woman comes begging, and having nothing else in the house to give her, he parts with the only copy of the New Testament they have. The liturgical lessons used to be read from it!

His life is full of the most delightful surprises of this kind – clinging tenaciously to the highest of ideals and then daring to make exceptions to them – even to the moment of his death. Lying on his deathbed, this fierce ascetic whose fasts and penances stagger one's very imagination has one last wish, to eat a piece of almond cake!

One cannot but marvel at the finesse with which he pulls off his feats of balancing on that fatally crucial edge. He is a dreamer who takes his dreams with tremendous earnestness and makes you sit on the edge of your chair anxious about the moment when he is going to slip off that rope and fall to his ruin; and then in that final split second when you think it has almost happened, there is that masterful shake of the head, and he is back on his feet, with a bow and a smile.

The Particular

But there is one thing more, and for me this is what makes him a true disciple of Christ. While he takes his dreams and ideals with daredevil seriousness and then with intuitive precision and humour just stops short of making them ultimate, there is something he does take with final and irrevocable seriousness, and that something is the individual and the particular.

Chesterton has dwelt at some length on Francis' interest in the particular and has pointed out that "to him a man was always a man and did not disappear in a dense crowd any more than in a desert", and that "he did not want to see the wood for the trees; he wanted to see each tree as a separate and almost sacred thing." Let us go back to that almond cake. Francis had been merciless in his self-denials and penances. Now on his death-bed he realizes that he has been too cruel to his body, "Brother Ass", and decides to pamper the beast a little. He thinks of his friend in Rome, the Lady Giacoma di Settisole, and writes to ask her to visit him and bring along the cloths and candles for his funeral – and also some almond cake. But he does not simply ask for the cakes, he adds, "like what you sometimes used to make for me when I visited your house." That little clause is Francis. What it contains of remembrance, appreciation and, above all, of courtesy is incalculable. And I do not know if in all of history there ever was a woman more proud of her cookies and of her hospitality than was Donna Giacoma till her dying day.

From the many other stories I pick out the one about that young novice who had been fasting and cried out in his bed from hunger one night. Fasting and penance had meant a great deal to Francis, for the Scriptures had insisted on them and the Lord himself had fasted often and it was by the same means that he, Francis, too had to master his own lower nature and follow his Master. For this reason he and the friars had made strict rules for themselves on fasting. But for a moment now all that disappears. Nothing exists for him on earth but this boy, hungry and shy. Any good superior would certainly have given him something to eat. But Francis sits down and eats with him! No analysis of the incident is necessary; one need only imagine the scene in all its loveliness – the dark kitchen and the candle light picking out the two faces with the jaws rising and falling and the muscle of the temple keeping rhythm, both men immensely grateful for the bread – and for each other.

This capacity to make exceptions and this preference for the particular over the collective, for the individual over the law and the common good, for the person over what are called higher values and ideologies, is what Francis learnt from the Gospel. Oddly enough this is something you cannot arrive at through logical processes. You have to become a fool. It involves a certain unreasonableness, a kind of short circuit in the brain. Like the foolishness of leaving ninety-nine sheep in the wilderness and going out looking for the one that has strayed. Or the folly of striking up the band and getting a celebration going with the fatted calf slaughtered, just because a good-for-nothing son who has wasted his fortune has come back home. Or the callous irresponsibility of bending down and writing with your finger in the sand while a host of accusers on fire with zeal for the law of Moses and the common good are waiting for your verdict on a bad woman. One can think of any number of reasons why this sort of behaviour should be banned and outlawed. In fact leaders of churches or other institutions have always been finding them, particularly at moments when the spirit and inner strength of the societies have been drained out and it occurs to them that law and order are the backbone of society. It is at such times that ideologies, rituals and laws become terribly important and assume an ultimate value. Prophets who come on the scene then, proclaiming the worth of the individual and trying to subordinate the Sabbath to Man, are promptly got out of the way. Either they are crucified, or placed in a niche high up, from where they can be comparatively harmless.

House of
Bernard of Quintavalle

©FM-'73

4 *A Sense of Humour*

I T HAS ALWAYS SEEMED to me that one of the most enchanting qualities of Saint Francis was his sense of humour. And this humour seems to be substantially no different from the humour of Jesus Christ. This had to be so, because Francis was the most ardent disciple of Jesus that ever lived, and Jesus was a man with a warm and profound sense of humour. All that Francis was he learnt from Jesus, and if we want to understand his sense of humour, we have to go to the Gospel.

Søren Kierkegaard said: "The Gospel represents the most humorous point of view in the history of the world." If in my own way I had to paraphrase the central core of the Gospel message as I understand it, and capture the heart and substance of the Good News in a few words, I think I would put it this way: "Have a sense of humour; for God's sake laugh!" This, I think, is what Jesus was trying to tell us all the time and it was mainly for saying this that they killed him. If he had preached only the love of God and the love of neighbour, prayer, fidelity to the covenant, charity to the poor and things like that, who knows they might have let him die a natural death, built a tomb for him and counted him among their great rabbis. But he asked them to laugh. That was too much!

Proportion

A sense of humour is a way of seeing, a way of facing the world and ourselves, a way of looking on everything as

59

relative. It is a readiness to see the ludicrous side of life. Fundamentally it is a sense of proportion, and it is this capacity that helps us to accept and live with what is incongruous. It does this by sparking off the explosive called laughter.

Laughter is one of the mysteries of human existence. I do not know if anyone can explain why exactly we laugh. Perhaps we could look for the reason in this direction: we are presented with reality on two planes. They look so much alike that we swallow them both, but then we see the incongruity, and are, so to say, forced to spit one out. This double process which is due to the mixing of congruity with incongruity bubbles over from the intellect into the body and tickles our ribs in some mysterious way. The result is a series of muscular contortions and convulsions ranging from the smile through the snigger, the chuckle and the guffaw to the side-splitting belly-laugh. The root of the whole mischief is this queer gift we humans happened to receive when we lost our tail, a sense of proportion.

When we see a man who is unusually short and fat, or unusually tall and thin, it makes us laugh, because we know what the proportions of a normal man are. A man who is pompous is funny, because we know there is no proportion between what he is and what he thinks he is. And when such a man steps on a banana skin it is even more funny, because the incongruity of it all becomes more obvious.

Humour also engenders sympathy, joy and other emotions that help us to become fully ourselves. When a cripple slips and falls we do not laugh, because it does not jolt our sense of proportion, it only stirs our compassion. And if the cripple should outshine the athlete, we laugh again and we rejoice, because that deep sense for the rightness of things tells us that another oddity of life has been righted.

People who are proud and pompous usually find it difficult to laugh, because, having an inflated opinion of themselves, they have their sense of proportion out of kelter. If they laugh it will be at things that boost their ego; they are incapable of that healthy and liberating sort of laughter – at themselves.

The Pharisees

The most influential leaders of the Jewish people at the time of Jesus, the Pharisees, were of this kind. Their capital sin was that they took themselves too seriously.

It was toward them that Jesus directed the major part of his sermons and parables and even his most harsh words. He never tired in his efforts to get them to have a good chuckle at themselves, because the essence of the message he came to teach concerned this very point.

When God gave the law to Israel through Moses, it was given in the context of a love-relationship. It was a covenant. In the second century before Christ there appeared a group of zealous people who called themselves the "Pharisees" (the Separated Ones), who made it their mission to see that the law was observed as perfectly as possible. They would observe not merely the law as given by Moses, but even the interpretations of it handed down by tradition. They hedged the law around with minute regulations so that the slightest breach of the smallest point was impossible. So here was a group of people who burned with zeal for the law and clung to it with a tenacity that would have surpassed Moses himself.

Except for one thing: they were holding it upside down. Instead of saying that because God accepted them and loved them God gave them the law as a charter of freedom and a gate to full living, they maintained that if they observed the law they would be accepted and loved by God.

They were placing an impossibly enormous burden on themselves, that of winning God's favour by their own efforts. By implication they were making themselves enormously important. By the observance of the law they could earn God's favour, they could acquire the right to be accepted by God, they could purchase God.

Here was a form of idolatry more subtle and more devastating than any the Old Testament had seen; the new golden calf was itself the idol, the sacrifice and the devotee.

This was no mere deviation from the scheme of things. It was a wrenching of the whole scheme out of the earth and planting it with roots in the sky and branches in the earth.

God's plan had been that human beings should come out of themselves and grow into the fulness of life in the sunlight of God's friendship. The whole process of growth was to be outward, skyward, into freedom and joy, with much laughter along the way. But the Pharisees would make it a gloomy affair, with man coiling around himself and developing into an ugly, gruesome thing.

Not an Employer

It is no wonder that Jesus came back on this point so insistently and so strongly as he did, and when everything failed, did not hesitate to use words that were harsh. He had to drill in the idea that God is not a taskmaster or employer from whom you have to earn your keep and whose goodwill depends on your performance, but he is your father, whose goodwill is already yours by the mere fact that you are his child, and who gives you what you need without your meriting it.

This concern of Jesus to present a true picture of his Father underlies many of his teachings. In telling us to learn from the birds of the air and the flowers of the field, he was certainly telling us to trust in God's providence and not be anxious about material goods. But this passage makes perfect sense also, and perhaps better, if we look at it against the background of the Pharisees' anxious care to look presentable before God and before others, and to store up merits for themselves. They are told to seek first God's Kingdom and God's righteousness and not their own, and God will take care of their good looks and their spiritual bank balance.

The obvious lesson contained in the parable of the Prodigal Son is that God's mercy is always ready to receive the repentant sinner. But it certainly has deeper layers of meaning. There is one character in it who emerges as a tragic figure as the story ends, the elder son. He is actually the Pharisee, the obedient "servant" who expects to be paid his dues: "These many years I have slaved for you," he says, "and I never disobeyed your command; yet you never gave me a kid that I might make merry with my friends." The father places the whole thing in perspective and points out the crucial value that what you *are* is more important than what you *do*: "Son, you are with me always and all that is mine is yours. But it was only right that we should celebrate and rejoice, because your brother here was dead and has come to life; he was lost and is found." We are not told whether the son came to share his father's sense of humour, had a good laugh at himself, embraced his brother and sat down to enjoy the veal with the music, dancing and laughter. Perhaps Jesus was leaving that to his listeners to decide, each one for himself (for we are all that son); he had a quaint way of doing that sort of thing.

In parable after parable Jesus pointed out that God's way of treating us does not depend on the excellence of our record of work, but on his infinite goodness. That was great good news indeed to all those who saw themselves for what they were really worth, namely very little. They could see how humorous the situation was: people who had worked all day were being paid no more than those who came at the eleventh hour; the sheep that had strayed and gone its own way was being carried home with song and laughter, while the ones that had behaved themselves had to walk home; the man who had bloated his pride with fasting, prayer and almsgiving had a puncture, while the publican who had nothing to rely on but the mercy of God was going home a friend of God; while the nobility who had received gold-lettered invitations to the royal wedding were making up their minds, the poor, the blind and the lame were taking their places at the wedding banquet and having a good time; prostitutes and bad characters were walking cheerfully into the Kingdom while the champions of the law were being told to wait outside. A funny world indeed! But the Pharisee could not see the joke. He had spent all his energies amassing merits for himself; he did not enjoy being told they were not going to be much use to him. This new teaching was shaking the foundations of the temple he had built to himself and that was something he did not appreciate. As far as he could see therefore, this was going to be the end of public morals and the decline of law and order in society. People would have no incentive to be good any more, or to work hard for their salvation.

But Jesus knew he was not advocating loose living or easy virtue. What he wanted most of all was to get the perspective right. The point of Jesus was that from his perspective there really aren't any of those ninety-nine good sheep in heaven; we are, every one of us, that hundredth sheep that strayed and is carried back on his shoulders; we are all that publican; we are all those poor, blind and lame who are made welcome in the banquet hall.

To accept the sonship given to you free for the mere fact that you are you, and to live out its implications was the glorious and joyous adventure Jesus was offering from God to all who would listen to him. To reject this sonship was sin.

Once this basic premise was established, there were great tasks indeed waiting for the child of God. No one could accuse Jesus of demanding too little of his followers. Both by precept and example he charged them with tasks that were superhuman.

I think it shows a great sense of humour on the part of a master and lawgiver to place on his disciples demands that are not only extremely difficult, but almost beyond their reach. It shows (and asks for) the ability to accept and to smile at the inevitable discrepancy between the ideal and the real, and yet keep striving for the ideal.

The laws and detailed regulations of the Pharisees were difficult to put into practice; but if you tried really hard, you could conceivably reach a stage when you could say, "I've done it, where's my pay?"

But love is an open-ended thing, and a law based on it can have no limits. When you are faced with demands like "love your enemies," "show the other cheek," or "love one another as I have loved you," no matter how hard you try, when evening comes you have to go back and say: "Lord, have mercy on me, a sinner." You are back where you started, in the home of your Father.

Before placing difficult demands on his listeners Jesus tells them how special they are and what capacities lie hidden in them: "If you love those who love you, what is special about that? Even pagans can do that. But YOU . . ." There is always something exclusive and a touch of family pride in the way he says "Your Father."

Risk

Jesus expects his followers to be always men and women of adventure, heroism and daring, and at home with risks and dangers. He was speaking not merely to those standing around but to every person in every age, in some situation of life, when he said: "Launch out into the deep," "Let us cross over to the other side," "You give them to eat," "Read the signs of the times," "Lazarus, come out!" "Let us go up to Jerusalem," "Go out into the whole world!" You cannot do such things if the most important thing in your life is to hold on to what you have got, either in the material or in the spiritual sense. You have got to learn to let go.

In the parable of the talents, there was one man who took great care not to lose his talent. He took trouble to bury it in the safest place possible and returned it intact. But he was the one who was punished. What went wrong with him was that he did not have a sense of humour; he took himself and his talent too seriously. He did not dare to take the risk of losing it, for he did not see it in the context of the whole story; he lacked a sense of proportion, he could not let go.

To know what is worthwhile when you see it and to risk everything for it is what the Kingdom is all about. And there is one more thing, the joy: "Then in his joy he goes and sells everything and buys that field."

The Laughter of Jesus

We see this joy and humour permeating the life of Jesus and singling him out of all the prophets of the Bible as the one who laughed most. His whole attitude toward life and all his teachings were so firmly founded on the bed-rock of God's fatherhood and unconditional acceptance of us, that his mirth had to spill over. There is a lovely, underlying humour in all his teachings and dealings with people, which every now and then bubbles up into laughter. I see him often suppressing a smile or a chuckle, or laughing out loud as he goes his way through the pages of the Gospel.

There is a great deal of humour in the way he tackles his adversaries and foils their plans to trap him in his words.

Particularly enchanting is the story of the woman taken in adultery, and the nonchalant way he sits and doodles in the sand while the accusers start slipping away one by one, "beginning with the eldest". And how masterfully and gently he pulls down the defences set up by the Samaritan woman. I would like to have seen his face when he said, "You are right in saying you have no husband . . ." At the wedding feast of Cana he tells his mother his time has not yet come; and in five minutes there are six jars of good wine going. One can imagine how he must have sat with an innocent face and enjoyed the joke when the steward started blaming the bridegroom for hiding the good wine till the last! In these and in many other stories, like those of the Syro-Phoenician woman, of Lazarus and of Jairus' daughter, there is an interesting sort of playfulness. Jesus lets the situation get as bad and hopeless as possible and almost out of hand, and then steps in and sets it right, making the whole Gospel story seem so much like an evening at the circus. The ultimate in this playfulness and the best practical joke he pulled off was the way he concluded the story by cheating death itself. His resurrection and the new life he brings to those who accept him in spite of their poverty and sinfulness are an eternal ridicule of the pomposity of the self-righteous.

Is it irreverent to talk in this way? I do not think so. "God laughs" said the psalmist (Ps. 2). In making us after God's own image and likeness, God gave us what no other creature was given, the gift of laughter. To me a Jesus who laughs is a lot more human (and no less divine) and a lot more lovable than a solemn and sombre-faced one. His humour is his most endearing quality. In Jesus, God laughs! Isn't that wonderful? Jesus' resurrection was part of God's laughter. It has the ingredients of many a fairy-tale and of the simplest of the stunt movies. The villain is big, has power, influence, everything. The circumstances favour him. He seems to be winning all the time. The plot moves to

67

a climax and in the last reel when he has almost made it, the tables turn, he is defeated, and the hero comes out on top. May we not laugh with God?

The Laughter of Francis

Laughing with God was what Francis was all about. Anyone who knows Francis cannot study the humour of the gospel without seeing where he picked up the tone of his laughter. Instances of Francis' humour are numerous enough to be treated on their own, but what is more important is the attitude of humour that underlies his whole life. Having grown up in a home where he knew what it meant to be totally accepted, he took his consciousness to a higher plane when he dramatically broke with his father, and, with that rare instinct for the essence of things, proclaimed: ". . . now I can truly say, Our Father in heaven". This basic and total acceptance of God as father and the gospel of Jesus as his rule of life brought about that tremendous capacity in Francis to laugh at himself and rejoice in his own littleness, the substance of his humour. Thus it was natural for him to laugh and sing in precisely those moments of life when most people would pity themselves. His joy was funny because it was so unexpected, it was an explosion. No wonder it has remained contagious to this day.

I see Francis as a little boy at the circus, fascinated with his Hero, and full of schemes on how he can go home and set up a circus too. He had to try out everything. If the great punchline of Jesus' life was his resurrection, he had his own punchline too; it was a brand new song: "Praise be to you, my Lord, for our sister, Death"!

5 Francis the Poet

T HERE ARE lots of sentimental people in the world, who can only associate Saint Francis with birds and rabbits and Brother Wolf. He will certainly forgive them if they like to look on him as a bleary-eyed romantic and the patron saint of languishing lovers of cats, dogs and parakeets.

No less ready would Saint Francis be, we can be sure, to forgive scholars who from their chairs of learning look down on any special attention paid to birds, flowers, sunsets or poetry in connection with him as sentimentality and blubber, and beneath their dignity.

It is a fact that all these things were part of his life, and they were there not merely in its periphery, but in its centre. They won't go away if you look the other way, nor can you put them in your little boxes and keep them alive. The sentimentalist who gets all worked up about them is missing the whole point of them, but so too is the scholar who either overlooks them benevolently as trivia, or studies them in their psychological and sociological depths, and stops short there. That would be like taking the pudding served up at table into your science laboratory and putting it through test tubes and under the microscope and producing pages of highly intelligent material and being satisfied with that. The whole point of poetry, and, we might say, of the Franciscan approach to learning itself, is that the proof of the pudding is in something else.

Saint Francis must be approached as a poet if he is to be understood at all. His life is full of images, colours and movements. All these must be seen as part of his personality. Isolated from it they become ridiculous – whether this isolating is done by sentimental superficiality or by deep scholarship.

Communication of Experience

A poem is not a piece of information, but the record of an experience in the depths of the poet. Part of that experience is his attempt to record it and share it. The words and allusions he has at his disposal, the capacities and limitations of the language, the cultural background, the rhyme and metre, if he uses them: all these he has to grapple with and make part of his experience. Even the use of a particular word because he needs it for rhyme or metre is part of the process. The poetic event is something beyond the control of the poet and has about it what commands reverence.

The poet or the mystic is a person who is more sensitive than the rest of us to the deeper realities of life. His senses perceive the same things as ours do, but suddenly he can be caught by what he perceives and shaken to his toes and left speechless. Speechless in the sense that the depth of the experience cannot be described in words or sounds or shapes or colours or anything. He is left with it to burn within him, while he helplessly struggles to give it expression.

It is different with the ordinary happenings of every day. They may be joyful or sad, and they may be important, even world-shattering, but they are prosaic in the sense that they do not touch the depths of life, they do not stir your roots. To communicate such things we have what is called prose.

Let us say you meet a friend and you would like to tell others about it. You can say, "I met so and so." You can describe

70

your meeting, you can say where you met him and how, and what he said and what you said. When you have described the whole incident, you have communicated the news.

The Birth of a Poem

But suppose you are walking in a meadow. Something you see or some train of thought suddenly sparks off in you a profound feeling of confidence in life, a feeling that no matter what happens, there is a presence that supports you, surrounds you and lifts you up, and in the most calamitous disaster will not forsake you. It could be an experience that so permeates your whole being that you stand there caught in its grip and lose all consciousness of time and surroundings. Then you come to yourself. The experience has made you so happy and so trustful that you want to share it with everyone. But how do you do that? You cannot describe it as you described your meeting with that friend. That was an incident and our human language had words to describe things like that. But where do you find words to describe the depths of what you have gone through? What you want to communicate is not an idea you have in your mind, but something your whole being has gone through and others have not. It is like wanting to describe the taste of ice-cream to someone who has never known it. You cannot give a scientifically accurate description. All you can do is to get him a cone. You cannot describe your experience to me in words, you can only try to evoke a similar one in me, or help me to call to mind snatches of similar experience I may have had. For this you would find yourself searching your memory and your imagination for pictures or stories. In desperation you might clutch at any straw that happens to be floating by. What you clutch at may be something picturesque, something colourful, or something weird or even foolish and ridiculous. For instance, you might think of yourself as a sheep, for you happen to be a shepherd living some thousands of years ago. You look at the sheep around you and the comfort and total abandonment they display. Suddenly you break into song: "The Lord is my shepherd, there is nothing I shall want." Where factual description was impossible, a fanciful image begins to succeed, at least partially. You are dealing with a reality that is far removed from sheep and shepherds, but that does not matter; the image was not meant to narrate what happened to you, but to suggest it and so to evoke a similar experience in others. You have broken away from normal ways of communication and, going further, broken away from normal speech. You are resorting to something that is quite a foolish way of communicating when you come to think of it; you have started singing.

Singing is a roundabout and slow way of saying things, quite inefficient from a business point of view. But you are not bothered about efficiency or about saving time. What you want is to celebrate. You have grasped an awesome truth with your hands, and you want to throw it about and jump around it and blow your horn and beat your drums till all the world has shared at least a bit of what you have seen with the eyes of your soul. You want to spread festivity around and you look about for colours. "How green are the pastures where he gives me repose." Your senses of touch and taste, your mouth, your gullet, your insides, everything must be called out to celebrate: "How cool, how fresh the waters, where he leads me to revive my drooping spirit." Panoramas open up before you, large vistas where you can roam, safe under his eye: "He guides me along the right path, he is true to his name." Then in your confidence you would like to throw down a challenge to all the powers of darkness and the very gates of hell: "If I should walk in the valley of the shadow of death, no evil would I fear. For you are there, and with your rod and your staff you give me comfort." You have exhausted your imagery, or rather your mind is so wild it goes looking for other pictures. Your enemies are going to be crushed and humiliated while you will have all you want and more. Here is a banquet hall lavishly spread and hung about with colourful festoons and flowers: "Envious my foes look on, while you spread a table for me." Being part of the culture of the ancient Middle East, you think of the oil on the head that brings coolness in the heat of the day, the oil of benediction flowing from the horn over the head of king and prophet, and, above all, the oil poured on the head of the guest which means welcome: "My head you have anointed with oil," and then that other sign of welcome, "my cup is brimming over." You come finally to the image of the house, that eternal symbol of security, peace and longevity: "Your goodness and love will be with me all the days of my life, your house will be my home for ever and ever."

God's Communication

Human beings need images, stories, myths, drama, song, colours, shapes, movements – in that unity of formal relations we call beauty – when we are faced with realities that are beneath the surface of life. Prose, which stands by us in all our mundane and pragmatic transactions, forsakes us the moment a sparkle comes into our eyes and our spirit tells us to launch out into the deep, and in a grain of wheat we see death and a resurrection, in a blade of grass hope and life, and in a woman carrying her child, all mothers, motherhood itself and the Madonna.

These experiences being too hot for us to touch with our bare hands and share with others, poetry and art in all their forms come to our aid as tongs to handle these burning coals. Prose informs, poetry evokes.

God sees this need of ours and so gives us the Bible, a book full of poetry, pictures, drama and colour. The way God speaks to us in the Bible is most picturesque and dramatic. There is a certain display of extravagance in the whole

73

communication that is worthy of the unapproachable
sublimity of the subject itself. God does not believe in what
is called economy of words. God is certainly not an expert in
brevity and terseness of speech, or in fast, efficient
communication. God is not the kind of person who would
send you a telegram in order to tell you something, but is
more likely to send you a special messenger who would be a
master story-teller (as Jesus was), a sensitive poet (as Jesus
was) and a man with a supreme sense of drama (as Jesus
was), who would have plenty of time to walk with you, to
stay with you, to eat with you and meanwhile to talk with
you so beautifully that your heart would be burning within
you all the time.

God is said to have given a brief and theologically precise
self-definition by saying to Moses on Mount Horeb, "I am
who I am." But that was not really a brief and precise
statement. What God actually said was much more. It was a
translation of the theological ideas (as we might call them) of
God's transcendence, unicity, omnipotence and supreme
glory into human terms. And the human terms God used
here were a mountain that had to be climbed, some square
feet on top of it that was holy ground, where you had to take
off your sandals, a bush in the middle of it that was on fire
without being burnt and which you were not allowed to
approach, and a splendour around it that made you cover
your face for fear of death. That was high drama indeed, and
splendid imagery and poetry.

Most of what God says in the Bible is said through events
and stories with a lot of panorama thrown in, and the
spoken or written messages of the prophets too are full of
pictures in colour and of cineramic proportions. The greater
part of the Scriptures was written by mystics and poets.
These, being specially equipped for a direct experience of
God, had to mediate this experience, and they could do that
only by means of poetry and drama.

Once the Scriptures were written, the dogmatic theologians and lawgivers moved in. They had to study the stories, parables, poems and metaphors of the Bible and distil the essential dogma that was in them. The unutterable had somehow to be uttered. Everything had to be translated into concepts and dogmas. This was a necessary process. The intellect is as much part of us as are memory, fantasy and the senses. And of all these faculties it is the one that gives you the surest grip on reality. Poetry can be vague, imagery can be ambiguous. So pictures, poems and stories have to be interpreted if we are to find out what exactly they mean. Thus the deposit of revelation which is contained in the Bible as seed has to sprout into theology, and theology has to grow in harmony with the sciences of every age, so that the eternal message of Scripture can be made relevant to all times.

The legitimate interst in speculative theology led to differences in interpretations and the growth of heresy. For protection of the true faith from heresy greater interest in theology was called for. Slowly the faith became more and more something that had to be defended and preserved rather than lived and celebrated.

When Francis of Assisi arrived, schools of learning had sprung up and masters of theology used to hold disputations. A lot of theology and scholarship was preached, which sailed above the heads of the common people. The most important things about being Christian were considered to be a good knowledge of correct dogma, intellectual assent to it and the practice of it in daily life.

The Message of Francis

But everything that was in Francis told him that Christianity was not something to be acknowledged and practised only, but something to be celebrated, to be sung about and danced about and made part of one's deepest experience.

75

The whole of scriptural revelation was a festivity and a celebration, and our response to it had to be nothing less. It had to go beyond understanding. God did not just tell us a lot of nice things about what it means to be divine and ask, "Do you agree?" but came out and took us by the hands, put loving arms around our shoulders, shook us all over, put a coloured mantle over us and a signet ring on our finger, brought us in, had the fatted calf slaughtered and the table laid, and got the music going.

Revelation had followed the dynamics of the dance. Dance is movement, and the only reasonable purpose of movement is to get from one place to another. But the dancer is quite unconcerned about that purpose. She turns, swirls and goes round and round, forgetting all about her destination. She is not in a hurry, she has time and enjoys wasting it. The purpose of the dance is movement itself, dance is a celebration of mobility and the beauty of the human body. God's self-revelation in the scriptures was not made so that we would listen, agree, practise and receive the reward of eternal life in heaven. Eternal life begins here, it is "to know you the only true God, and the one you have sent, Jesus Christ" (John 17:3). This knowledge, which is not a matter of the intellect only, but of the whole being, is a dialogue and is its own purpose, something that deserves celebration. God had started this celebration and Francis wanted to join in.

The dogmatic theologians had translated this poetry into prose, this experience into dogma – a legitimate and helpful process, but quite pointless if it did not lead to a deeper, religious experience, and fraught with awful dangers. It could twist you around itself and make you believe that was religion. This was a worse temptation than the temptation to lust or greed, for theology was no sin, it had its functions. It therefore made it easier to indulge one's intellectual prowess and lead oneself to believe one was being religious. The sin of the fornicator and the murderer was bad, but that of the Pharisee was worse. And not a few clerics of Francis' time had been caught in this whirlpool. That was why Francis discouraged learning among his followers. But he did not despise theology; he just saw it as far inferior to the kind of knowledge he himself had of God and he wanted his brothers to taste the real thing. Nor did he despise theologians; in fact he greatly honoured and revered them. In his letter to St Anthony he appoints him to teach theology to the brothers, adding that the spirit of prayer and devotion should be kept alive. Whatever may be said about the authenticity of the letter, the Franciscan approach to learning is certainly reflected there. A theologian who prayed as Anthony did and could move people to devotion the way he did could certainly negotiate the whirlpool.

But for himself Francis preferred the direct approach to God through poetry and drama, not only because that was God's way of approaching us, but because that was the only way the immensity of the gulf could be bridged and the contact made. Being naturally endowed with a keen sense of drama, he was awed by the supreme drama of God approaching us and even becoming one of us. He never quite got over that. And he was fascinated by the fact that in that entire process of self-emptying God had adapted himself to our way of thinking, spoken our language. Bethlehem, Calvary and the Eucharist were highly dramatic manifestations and language we could understand. Francis wanted to enter into these poetic phenomena and experience the union that God was reaching out with.

Poetry can be understood only with the heart, it calls for an "empathy", a feeling into. You have to let go of the security of pragmatism, efficiency and clarity of concepts and become a fool. You have to join in the play.

The Poetry of Francis

Seeing God made small and poor in human form, the dramatist and poet in Francis takes out a begging bowl and walks through the streets. The more insults he receives the more he enjoys it, for he is in great company. He tells his brothers, "Do not ever be ashamed of begging, for the Lord made himself poor for us in this world."

He reads in St Paul's letter to the Corinthians the scenic description of the Israelites traversing the desert, and drinking water from the rock, and is fascinated by St Paul's footnote-like remark, "and the rock was Christ". He is not satisfied with merely relishing the poetry of it, but wants to join in. He acts out his reaction. The Document of Perugia says it with affection and tenderness: "When he had to walk on rock, he did so with fear and reverence, for love of him who is called the Rock."

There was the time when his attraction for contemplation and prayer was so strong that he thought of giving up preaching altogether. He prayed for God's guidance but did not want to trust his own lights on God's answer. He called Brother Masseo and asked him to go to Sister Clare in San Damiano and Brother Silvester in his mountain cave on Subasio with the request that each of them take a companion and pray to God to show them what to do. We see Francis now waiting at the door of the Portiuncula for Masseo's return. The verdict he brings will shape his whole future – and looking from our stance we can see, the future of the entire Franciscan movement. Suddenly a thought strikes him: Masseo will be carrying God's word for him; how gracious of God to deign to reveal the divine will to him, Francis, the little worm that he is! And how magnificent that God should do that through his Brothers and Sisters! Lights now begin to flash and the depths of his soul are stirred and shaken. He finds himself in the grip of a mystical experience of profound wonder and reverence for the word of God and of love and gratitude toward his community of Brothers and Sisters, whose words will reveal this word to him. He wrestles with this experience. How is he to come to terms with it?

The mystic can cope with his world only by turning into a poet, a singer, an actor. Through the woods in the distance the figure of Masseo is seen approaching. Francis takes a vessel of water and goes up to receive him. He tells him not to speak yet, and then kneels down and washes his feet. Did not Isaiah say, "How beautiful upon the mountains are the feet of him who brings good tidings!"? Then his scriptural memory flies back a few centuries and sees Abraham and Gideon receiving God or God's messenger. He tells Masseo to wait, goes into the kitchen and prepares a meal for him and brings it with reverence. I once walked from San Damiano to the Portiuncula through the fields (which were forests in Francis' times), trying to follow Masseo, and can well imagine he was hungry, what with that extra length from Mount Subasio as well, and relished the repast.

When Masseo has eaten, he takes him into the woods to a spot he specially loves. He does not want to receive him in his hut, which is certainly not more worthy than the house of the centurion. There, in the cathedral of that forest, Francis bares his head of the cowl, kneels down before Masseo, crosses his arms and says, "What does my Lord Jesus order me to do?" Masseo replies, "To both Sister Clare and Brother Silvester the Lord has given the same reply: he wants you to go about the world preaching, for he did not call you for yourself alone, but also for the sake of others." Francis jumps to his feet and says, "Then let us go, in the name of the Lord!" The *Fioretti* says that he "set out like a bolt of lightning in his spiritual ardour, paying no attention to road or path". He goes to Cannara and preaches so fervently that the whole population wants to abandon the village and follow him. It is also on this occasion that he preaches to the birds, so great is his eagerness to do the Lord's bidding.

The whole incident is pure poetry acted out. It is memory and fantasy running wild and throwing a celebration because there is no other way to get hold of and assimilate that spiritual experience of receiving the sizzling word of God from the mouth of Masseo. The immediacy of his action is not due to scrupulosity or some exaggerated notions of obedience, but is his way of spreading the red carpet to welcome the Word.

To narrate all that was poetic and dramatic in Francis' life would be to write his entire biography. There was nothing he touched which did not stand up and sing. Poetry was something he lived.

His passion for taking things literally, "without gloss, without gloss", was also part of this attitude. He was too much of a poet to be satisfied with conceptual interpretations.

When the crucifix of San Damiano said to him, "Francis, go and repair my house!" it was the most natural thing for him to take it literally and do it in the most obvious manner. It would have been most unlike Francis to analyze its meaning there and see larger implications in the sentence. It was because he took it literally, as he took the whole Gospel literally, and repaired that particular church that he was able to fulfil it figuratively and repair the tottering Church of his time.

These aspects of Francis' life are easy enough to understand, but are difficult for our age to enter into and become part of. Ours is an age that is a little shy of these things, because they belong to the area of life that is useless.

The Useless

Most of the things we do in our life have a use and a purpose to fill. Such are working, earning, eating, resting, travelling, etc. But what makes life livable and gives meaning and depth to it is the area of it that is useless. Poetry, art, religion, ritual and celebration belong to this area. We indulge in these activities not to achieve something but because unconsciously we feel the need to touch the roots of our being and of our common humanity.

If you talk of the sun rising as the giant preparing to run his course, it is not because that is a more useful way of putting it, but because the sight of the sunrise makes you want to leap out of the humdrum of life and touch a truth that is transcendental. It is for the same reason that the sun becomes Brother Sun.

In an age when rationalism, positivism, technology and a materialistic outlook on life have geared all human activity to hard work, efficiency and achievement, it is only to be expected that celebration, play, ritual and poetry are left to the specialists. People prefer watching these on the screen or on television as a means of diversion, rather than being participants.

A civilization whose mottos are: "Nothing succeeds like success" and "Time is money" cannot be expected to understand what the fox said to the Little Prince in Antoine de Saint-Exupéry's famous book: "And now, here is my secret, a very simple secret: it is only with the heart that one can see rightly; what is essential is invisible to the eye . . . It is the time you have wasted on your rose that makes your rose so important."

A Franciscan Task

In times such as ours the disciples and lovers of Francis carry an awful burden: that of repairing the Church by incarnating

81

in their lives, and of helping others to incarnate in theirs, the approach of Saint Francis to the deepest realities of life. It is difficult because so many things have changed since his times, but is none the less imperative because so many have not.

Take for instance Francis' profound reverence for the word of God. One quaintly charming and highly poetic way in which he expressed it was by keeping his eyes open for any pieces of paper that might be lying about on the road while he walked along. He would go and pick them up. Sometimes it happened to be a piece discarded by some careless copyist after writing some line from the Bible to try his quill. Francis would then dust it carefully and take it with him with reverence and keep it in some suitable place. Oddly enough Saint Francis considered this act of his to be so natural that in his *Letter to a General Chapter* he asked all the brothers to do it, and came back on it again in his Testament.

Today, after the invention of printing, especially of mechanized printing, a gesture like that cannot have the same meaning; it would be neither poetic nor eloquent as it was with Francis, but merely ridiculous. But what we can do is to look around with Francis' eyes and his reverence for the word. If our fantasy is fed on images from the scriptures like his was, we shall find any number of ways to embody and act out that reverence in our world relevantly today. We shall find that there is a way of holding the Bible or keeping it on the table that shows how precious it is, a way of printing it and binding it and a way of making a stand for it that show it is worth more to us "than heaps of gold and silver pieces"; a way of reading it in public (certainly not from a sheet of paper, but from the leather-bound, gold-laced book itself) and a way of raising our voice and speaking the words out that show we understand our responsibility to make the word come alive to the congregation, a responsibility that made Moses, Isaiah and Jeremiah shudder. We shall also then realize that reading the scriptures in church is not a utilitarian act like driving a nail or scrubbing a floor but a celebration. If we see it merely as an act with a purpose, the purpose of getting the intellectual contents of the text into the brains of the listeners, we reduce it to a prosaic thing. Then it becomes important that the listeners be provided with printed sheets or books so they can follow and understand. But if the reading is a celebration of the community, then on the one hand it calls for loud, clear and lively enunciation (people who cannot do this should not be called upon to read), and on the other, attentive listening. From a passive half-activity which requires reinforcement from the printed text in the hand, listening would then become an active welcoming of the word, something worth doing in itself as part of a joyous drama that unites the community in a single act. The act of reading and the act of listening would then become important as acts of prayer and reverence for the word rather than a preparation for prayer.

If in this way we develop an eye for the poetic aspects of Francis' life – for the gestures and images that came so naturally to him, and learn to be part of them and share in some small way in the deeper experiences that are the heart of the poet he was, we shall find many other areas too in our own life today and in that of the Christian community that can be enormously enriched. That is a kind of enrichment and deepening the Church needs today more than ever before.

Man for our Times

At least partly the crisis in faith and worship the Church is passing through today has been traced to an over-intellectualization of the Christian faith that started soon after the Roman persecutions and received its great boost with the invention of printing and the use made of it by Luther and Canisius and the scholastic theologians, and reached its peak in the age of rationalism. God's revelation to man in the Scriptures, which was an "audio-visual", multi-sensory message with poetic effusions and dramatic images, came to be crystallized into concepts and distinctions and explanations. Slowly the Christian Church forgot what it meant to think and feel by means of image and sound.

In our own times the results of this can be seen in some new versions of the Bible and the translations of the ICEL in which little appreciation is shown for imagery or poetry. In the centurion's prayer before communion at the mass the lovely and rich image of the house and the roof which are unworthy for the Lord to enter are wiped out and replaced with the clear, efficient and prosaic "I am not worthy to receive you!"

Pope John XXIII.
at the tomb of Saint Francis
before the opening of the
Second Vatican Council,
4 October 1962

A Church with such an impoverished sense for the picturesque and the imaginative is suddenly faced today with a culture where people are simply surrounded and massaged by sense perceptions through the electronic media. A new generation that has grown up on television, radio, cinema, posters and picture magazines, and has learned to do most of its thinking through pictures and sounds, colours and rhythm, like the people of the Biblical times, looks to a Church that has forgotten this kind of language. It is just beginning to learn it again.

The greatest watershed in this re-learning process of the Church in modern times has been the Second Vatican Council. In the week preceding the solemn opening of the Council in October 1962 there happened a small incident which has gone largely unnoticed, but should have significance for all lovers of Saint Francis. To pray for the success of the Council, Pope John XXIII, its central figure, made a pilgrimage to a shrine of our Lady and to a tomb. Of all the thousands of tombs of saints in Italy he chose, with that rare sense for the symbolic, the tomb of Saint Francis in Assisi. There he prayed that just as he repaired and rebuilt the tottering Church of the thirteenth century, Francis might repair and rebuild ours too.

Francis of Assisi calls us, followers of Christ and carriers of God's word for our age, to learn once again the poetry of God and meet him in the explosion of his joy, which is creation. He tells us that the centre of the human being is not the brains but the heart, that his imagination, memory and feelings are part of him too. He shows us what we all knew in our cradles, but forgot, that colours have tongues, that hands can shout and fingers sing, that feet have a language of their own, that trees do clap their hands and mountains skip like rams, that sun, moon and stars, air and clouds, water, fire and earth are members of our family and singers in our chorus.

City wall near
Porta Nuova

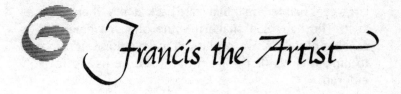

6 Francis the Artist

A CERTAIN RELATIONSHIP with matter, it seems to me, is one fundamental element that goes into the making of an artist. He has to love it, become part of it and make it part of himself, speak to it and listen to it with tenderness and reverence, if he is to be able to make it the vehicle of his inner vision without destroying its life and character. The inner vision is, of course, the soul of what the artist is, be he the poet who works with words, the dancer who works with movement, the sculptor with stone or wood, the musician with sound and time, or the painter with pigments. But besides that there has to be this deep love and reverence for the material he works with. Without it his vision and message would not ring true, no matter how much skill and expertise he may bring to the work.

Saint Francis seems to me to be the one man in whom this quality of the artist is supremely present. His approach to beauty is part of his spirituality no less than his prayer life or poverty or penance, and cannot be ignored if we are to understand him and present his message to a world that so badly needs it.

This is a subject that is easy enough to fantasize and visualize and sing about. But how may we approach it with words and concepts and try to understand it?

Things and People

Let us look at a baby with his first toy in his hand, a rattle. The toy has a handle with a good grip and a head with two large eyes painted on it that stare back at him when he stares at it. The baby can shake it – the only movement he is capable of right now – and it will make a noise. It *responds* to him. It is his first grip on the world he has so recently entered.

When he was born, in that confused jumble of sensations and experiences, the one clear impression that predominated in his brain was that he was the centre of the world. The whole universe was created exclusively for him. He was important. Surveying his realm as the weeks and months went by, he slowly began to distinguish two categories of subjects – people and things. People responded, things did not. He saw himself surrounded by people – people who hugged him, talked to him, did terrible things to him like bathing him and wiping him with towels. He smiled at them and they smiled back at him. If he was uncomfortable or needed anything, all he had to do was open his mouth and let out a yell, and they were there ready to do anything in the world to make him happy. He could relate to them. It is this response that draws the child out of himself to become human; in his discovery of people he discovers himself.

Alongside of people who respond to him, the child goes on to discover things. Here is a thumb that is nice to suck all day, here are fingers, toes, bedsheets, buttons, all kinds of things. But the distinction is still vague in his mind, he thinks that he can relate to things the same way as he can relate to people. What he has in his hand in that rattle is a thing, but it responds.

As he grows older the distinction becomes clearer and clearer, but he still finds it meaningful to keep a certain vagueness about it, and to treat objects as if they were people. That is the rationale behind the toy. A rattle becomes a fascinating thing, dolls become real personalities with names, with whom he can hold serious conversations.

But the child is not cheated into believing that the dolls are real people. He knows he is pretending, but finds it good to pretend. Something within tells him that his being grows when it relates and interacts, be it with people or with things. He presumes "graciousness" in everything and is friendly with animals, and the animals, with their instinctive feeling for innocence, usually respond, as if in remembrance of the long lost days of paradise. The child's trust and vulnerability make him the friend of all the world.

Sin

But as he grows up he begins to perceive evil in the world around him and in himself. He begins to lose his innocence and with that comes fear, and with fear new defences. The dolls are replaced with tin soldiers and pistols, symbols of defence, and afterwards with weapons of defence and self-assertion, be they transistors, long hair, slogans or drugs. He has stopped *relating* to things and now *uses* them. This is a legitimate part of growth, but he has to be guided in this development. If not, the loss of innocence continues, and he eventually reaches the extreme in which he uses even people. Things become mere things, shorn of all the human values he had endowed them with earlier. Then people too become things, shorn of these values – all to be used for his own purpose. This is the essence of sin and the root of mental pathology. Man stops relating and makes himself the master and manipulator of the world.

That in fact is the meaning of the story of paradise in the Book of Genesis. At first man lives in harmony there – with others, with the beasts and with the material universe. The earth is his friend. But he tries to use the forbidden fruit to make himself the centre and become God. With that the harmony is broken and he becomes a stranger to the earth and all creation, to his fellows and to himself. And thus to God.

Such is the world we are born into, a world where sin comes easy, where we are collectively guilty of estrangement.

A Reconciled World

The kingdom Jesus came to proclaim and to inaugurate is a reconciliation deep down in the human soul – a restoration of peace with the whole created universe, with one's neighbour, with oneself, and thus with God. Jesus was himself this reconciliation in its completeness; in him God and man met and became one – one person who, while he is God, is brother to all people and the First-Born of all creation. He took matter and re-created it by making it part of himself, in a body with shape, colour, weight and smell like any other.

As he pondered the mystery of this kingdom in his mind to teach it to his brothers and sisters and share its secrets, it took shape in the images of the humble objects of the earth – the grain of wheat, the tree, the flower, the birds of the air, the fish of the sea, the colours of the sky, the blowing of the winds, the movements of clouds and rain, fire and water, and the dark brown earth.

The means he chose as vehicles to hand this reconciliation to all people to the end of time, were also the simple things of nature, matter in its crass, everyday existence – water, salt, oil, breath of air, sound of words, wheat baked into bread and grapes pressed into wine.

Francis

Francis of Assisi stands in history as the one man in whom this reconciliation took place in nearly as perfect a manner as is given to a mere human. Through hard, persistent struggle with the forces of evil within and delicate sensitivity to the whisperings of the Spirit, he achieved, or rather, allowed God to achieve within him, an abundance of peace with God, with his fellows and with himself: this abundance had to overflow to the material universe and to hold all created objects, from the sun and the moon, to the worm by the wayside, and even death, in a sweeping fraternal embrace. Having regained paradise in the depths of his soul in this way, it was the most natural thing for him to go up and have a little chat with the wolf that was ravaging the countryside and gather him into the brotherhood of Eden, where he happily lies down in peace with house-dogs. Or to preach a homily to the birds and have them sit and listen quietly till he has finished. There was a certain playfulness combined with sincere reverence in the way he treated fire and water – those elements so necessary for human life, yet capable of such devastation and havoc – and they returned his courtesy. His companions and early biographers saw the disarming simplicity and fairy-tale quality of these and many such instances as part of the larger story of Francis' return to paradise and to the innocence of childhood. The world became for him a large playpen filled with toys and dolls of all kinds that he could play with and talk to in all earnestness.

Beauty a Ladder?

Michelangelo said, "My soul can find no staircase to heaven unless it be through the earth's loveliness". He loved marble and he loved the human form and celebrated the beauty of these. He gave soul to stone as few men on earth have done. He was an artist and he took the beauty of the world with great seriousness – not as a means to the end of loving God, but as good in itself – and found it led him to God.

But when a saint says a thing like that he leaves himself open to the suspicion that actually he cares for nothing but God, and that the beauty of the world is for him only an object to be used for reaching God. In fact Francis' early biographers, who devote considerable attention to the way he related to animals and to the material universe, make it a point to state most of the time that it was God's beauty he saw in them and his glory that he praised. "In every work of art," says Celano "he praised the Artist; whatever he found in things made he referred to the Maker . . . He made for himself from all things a ladder by which to come close to his throne."

To infer from this that God was all that mattered to Francis and everything else mattered only as a reminder of God and as a tool in his hand for praising God would be to miss the real point of Francis' approach to creation.

God was indeed the central point of Francis' relationship with the material universe, but not in the sense that things lost their identity and value in themselves, and became mere instruments in the practice of religion. Nothing could have been farther from Francis' attitudes. One of the most charming aspects of his character was that he took everything with great seriousness. For him things were important in themselves, and that meant they were important also in their relationships.

The Aesthetics of Francis

Reaching out to all created things in depth and taking them seriously for what they were in themselves, Francis had thus to take them in the way they related to one another, and to all reality. He then found that the greatest of their relationships, the one that gave them most meaning and dignity, was their dependence on God. Their most significant value was that their ultimate roots touched the wellspring that is God in the same was as his own did. Thus he stumbled upon an astonishing discovery, that if things were important in themselves, they were not only related one to another, they were also his own relatives – they were his brothers and sisters. God, being the ultimate ground of this cosmic home, was part of every one of these relationships. Thus the more Francis took things seriously and loved and respected them for their own sakes, the more God came into his relationship with them. The totality of his surrender to God was not compromised, but rather enhanced, by the pleasure he took in relating to creatures.

This brought about in him an abundance of that harmony of relationships that is called sanity of mind. It accounts for the great joy and playfulness we find in Francis' attitude toward creatures. That quaint way he had of talking to animals and even to inanimate objects and calling them Brother and Sister was no sentimentality or cheap romanticism. It was a poetic dramatization of the way he felt deep down about things. "Brother" and "Sister" were theological terms for him. They indicated that nothing created – from the farthest star to the lowest insect – was too small or unimportant to be part of an in-depth relating and profound communion, grounded on the Fatherhood of God.

The deep reverence he had for all creatures was thus part of his poverty – his total and joyful acceptance of his creatureliness before God. He embraced poverty with the ardour of bridal union. The heroic hardships he imposed upon himself as part of this poverty were not its soul but only its expression. Its soul was the relationship with God in which he totally accepted and celebrated his dependence on him. The completeness of this acceptance and celebration required that he place himself in the long and humble row of his fellow-creatures and mingle with them in brotherly communion.

This communion had to be a serious and reverent affair, because God was part of it. Rocks and mountains, streams and rivers, everything had to be treated with respect, because they were all part of the cosmic harmony whose centre was Christ. He could not think of doves or lambs or worms without thinking of Christ, for Christ was the bond that tied them to each other and to him. Everything reminded him of Christ, for Christ was the First-Born of all creation, the Prime Model from which everything was fashioned. Later Franciscans were to develop this into the theology of the primacy of Christ, but the seeds of it are to be found in the way he spoke to Sister Cricket and asked her to sing, or pleaded with Brother Fire to be kind to him during the cautery of his temples, or stopped and picked up a worm on the path lest someone should stamp on it.

Because things were important in themselves, God had to come into the picture, and when God came in they became doubly important. So when Francis responded to the beauty of the created world, what he saw first was the beauty of the things being themselves. For him water was important because it was water, and birds were important because they were birds. His attitude towards beauty was based on the intrinsic goodness of things. It was "other-centred" and therefore based on respect. "In beautiful things he saw Beauty itself; for him all things were good," says Celano.

Fake Beauty

Quite out of keeping with the aesthetics of Francis is the phoney appreciation of beauty that we are getting used to in this technological age of ours. It is being made increasingly easy for us now to look for beauty in a way that is centred not in the objects but in ourselves. Instead of appreciating the beauty of a thing in its being itself, we are made to take it as beautiful merely because of the impression it makes on the retina of our eyes. This approach is not only superficial, but the exact opposite of the other-centred and respectful attitude of Saint Francis.

Mechanical duplication, while it has been a great step forward in man's conquest of nature, has brought its own retribution in that it has dulled our sensitivity to the material universe and our capacity to relate to nature. Wood, for instance, is an intrinsically beautiful thing, so is marble.

Their beauty lies not in the grains and veins they display on their surface, but in the fact that these are within them as well and are part of their nature. These tell us stories of the life and growth of the wood and put us in touch with the eons during which nature shaped and coloured the marble. What we see on the surface is what is within, and no two surfaces are the same. The appearance leads us to the core of the substance and our whole being responds to the whole being of the object, and we come to a rapport with it. A table made of genuine teakwood, for instance, becomes thus not merely an object that serves your convenience and helps you to work, but also an object with a "soul" of its own, to which you can relate. A marble slab becomes not just a thing that can be of use to you, but also something with an intrinsic worth, something with a character of its own, quite different from that of granite or cement. You can establish communion with these objects as you use them. While you respect them for their God-given dignity, the communion helps you to grow into a fuller humanity.

Then technology comes along and brings you laminated sheets, which look exactly like these materials. They have photographed the surfaces of wood and marble, printed that on paper and pressed that between sheets of highly-polished, heat-resistant, scratch-resistant, unbreakable etc., etc., substance. You can now have your table made of cheap wood, or factory-made planks of compressed wood-shavings or anything else and have the top lined with the highly efficient laminated sheets that fake the surface of wood, and tell yourself: "Isn't it beautiful?" What you are doing is allowing your idea of what is beautiful to depend on what impression it makes on your eyes and senses and not on what it is in itself. Here is a counterfeit relationship, or rather, no relationship at all. People who can live and work comfortably with furniture of this kind are people who have never learnt to relate to real wood or marble in depth.

People who are comfortable with artificial flowers and can pray with those on the altar, are people who have not been able to take time for genuine flowers or to commune with them. Of course, one can admire these imitation flowers or wood or stone for the ingenuity and skill that have gone into their manufacture, but for all that they remain "dead" objects, and their sin is in the fact that they pretend to be what they are not. Paper flowers can be works of art and beautiful if they *do not pretend* to be natural flowers, but are made to look artificial, and so are themselves. Lies should have no place in our worship, or in our lives. Insensitivity to this sort of falsehood and inability to see through it all is what our technology has given us as its special legacy.

Setting the Universe Free

What has taken place in a very subtle manner here, as in a host of similar cases, is a return to the state of unredeemedness. St Paul says that "creation itself will be set free from its bondage to decay and obtain the glorious liberty of the children of God . . . The whole of creation has been groaning in travail together until now" (Rom. 8:21-2). The redemption that Jesus brought us and the "glorious liberty of the children of God" have to be extended to the whole of creation. This is the task of redeemed mankind. We have to set the universe free. We can see two aspects to this liberation of matter, the technological liberation and the theological one. The first is the task of every human being. It means setting free the immense powers for good that the Creator has invested matter with. The discovery of fire, of electricity and of atomic power were such liberations. Science and technology have been engaged in this liberation from the beginning of history and have been pursuing it with ever-increasing vigour.

But the more important liberation is what we could call the theological one, which is the task of every Christian, and still more, or everyone who tries to follow Saint Francis. This is a liberation that we have to bring about not in the objective realm of things themselves, but within us. We bestow this liberation on matter by re-structuring our attitudes and our approach to it in the light of God's revelation in Christ. We do that when we approach matter as being valuable in itself and deserving of our respect and wonder for its intrinsic dignity as our fellow-creature before God. By sin Adam sundered all the relationships that existed between himself and the created universe. All the bonding cords lay disrupted, like a giant telephone exchange with all the connections gone haywire. We have to restore to things their intrinsic worth by repairing these connections within us.

In the introduction to his book *Saint Francis* Nikos Kazantzakis says, "For me Saint Francis is the model of the dutiful man, the man who by means of ceaseless, supremely cruel struggle succeeds in fulfilling our highest obligation, something higher even than morality or truth or beauty: the obligation to transubstantiate the matter which God has entrusted to us, and turn it into spirit."[1] A great artist with words in our own times, Malcolm Muggeridge, affirms the same thing in a different way when he says, "Making the Word flesh and vesting it with grace and truth . . . this is what every artist is endlessly seeking to do."[2] They are talking of one form of liberation that man bestows on material things, capturing the spirit in them and making them sharers in the glorious freedom of the children of God, the task that Francis performed with such consummate skill in and by his life.

When Michelangelo carved the face of Christ in marble in his *Pietà* he was transubstantiating stone and turning it into spirit, he was making the Word flesh and vesting it with grace and truth. Francis was doing much the same thing, and in a higher sense, when he "walked on rock with fear and reverence for love of Him who is called the Rock".

Art in its essence is the transubstantiating of matter, the enfleshing of the Word in it, and must rise as much from an authentic respect for and rapport with matter as from the vision of the other world. An undying passion for authenticity and search for the inner personality of every material must mark the artist and anyone who would want to live a full life the way Francis did.

A watercolour that looks like an oil painting is a bad watercolour. An oil painting that looks like a photograph is a poor work of art. A wood carving must respect and take into account the grains and inner character of wood. It would be sinning against its own nature if it pretended to be (that is, if the sculptor made it pretend to be) a work in marble.

This respect is a spiritual attitude and a Christian way of looking at matter, not something meant for artists only. It is a way of seeing. We can carry it into all our relating with matter. The result will be an enriching of our own selves and a fuller sharing in the maturity of Christ and in his redeeming of the material universe.

Estrangement

Seen from Francis' point of view, the malaise of our civilization appears to be traceable to its estrangement from Mother Earth – earth in the larger sense of all matter and nature itself. This estrangement carries its price-tag. The farther we move from nature the more we stand to lose of our humanity – if we are not extremely careful.

What modern printing technology, in collaboration with photography, can come up with is astounding. In a matter of hours printers can run off thousands of copies of a Rembrandt masterpiece perfect to its smallest nuance of colour, so that people who otherwise would never have a chance of seeing a Rembrandt can study it in their rooms, thousands of miles away. That is the good part. But the not-so-good part is that the painting becomes de-personalized. The wonder, awe and reverence you feel before an original Rembrandt, which has come from the hand of the master and is the only one of its kind in the world and with which your soul can commune, is taken away. The masterpiece becomes a mere arrangement of colours on paper. It is shorn of its personal element and becomes a mere thing – one of thousands produced by a machine. You can study it, but not relate to it.

Or take electronics. What people can do with sound production today is breath-taking. Its benefits for pleasure and education are incalculable. That is the good part. But the retribution it carries is this: music becomes not only depersonalized, but what is worse, is deprived of its character as an *event*. And when music is not an event it becomes sound, or worse, noise, a succession of waves, possibly good enough for analysis or study or for background decoration.

In the old days if you wanted to play music you had to study and practise for years. Even to listen to good music you had to take trouble; you had to dress up and go to a concert hall. It was a pilgrimage in which reverence was an intrinsic element. There were the rituals – the tuning up, the announcements, the arrivals of the leader of the orchestra and of the conductor. Then it was a moment of grace when the thousands of people in the hall held their breath and in that sacramental silence the maestro lifted the baton and the first notes began to sound. Today you can make music by pressing a button and you can carry the choir and the entire orchestra in your pocket.

Deprived of this *event* aspect, music often becomes a background or lubricant to conversation, and sometimes, as at parties, the background can be made louder so that the conversation can remain on a superficial level. People have lost their capacity to *listen* – to listen to the music event, to

99

listen to one another, and to listen to themselves. We have become de-humanized.

Positively

We cannot stifle technology, that wonderful gift God has given us through human hands. It would be a sin to despise it. But we can prevent it from making us less human and slaves of the monster called "More Convenient".

What we need is to have our values in their proper order and to be discriminating in the use of technology. Reverence, wonder, humour, authenticity – these values must never be allowed to erode.

In our enjoyment or teaching of art and music, the use of photography, printing and electronics can be a great help, and is even indispensable today. But the price of keeping our human values is eternal vigilance. We have to keep clearly before us the difference between an original and a print, a handmade object and a machine-made one – not losing sight, of course, of academic artistic values, which means that a reproduction of a good work of art might be preferable to a bad original. Music is greatly impoverished (and greatly impoverishes) if we do not see it as an event. Even in listening to recorded music we can create a new event and become part of it. That means we have to make listening a serious activity, an active human process in which we are fully ourselves, not something we pay half attention to while talking. Thus in the use of technology we have to keep our balance and never let it blunt our sensitivity to the divine Presence deep down in the nature of things.

Patron of Ecology

Ecology, with Saint Francis as its patron, should mean much more to us than conserving the natural resources of the earth and halting the pollution of sea and sky. I think artificial flowers, electric candles and imitation wood are ecological sins just as the devastation of forests and the extermination of wild life are. They dehumanize us no less. Our immediate environment is as important as our larger environment. Preserving the wilderness of the earth is grand. But what point would it have if we did not know how to relate with respect to the wood in a matchstick as our fellow-creature?

Francis calls us to this kind of relating. He has lessons to give us on how to use our eyes and how to use our ears – not merely to see and hear with but to put our deeper selves in contact with the sanctuary of God in the heart of things.

Why anyone should pay so much attention to this aspect of Francis' spirituality is something that cannot be demonstrated and proved. If you want to understand why it is important, there is only one way, and it is this: on a dark night gather some dry wood and light a fire, sit before it and stare into it, don't try to think anything, don't even try to pray in the usual sense, but just sit and look; *waste time* with it, listen with your heart to what it is trying to say. On a hot, sunny day wash your face under a tap of cold water, and see if it talks to you. On a cold day, when the sun is high, close your eyes and face the sun; let the rays caress your face and contact your soul. Take a stone in your hand, just big enough to be a handful, look at it, feel all around it with both your hands, weigh it, throw it in the air and catch it, try to reach its character and understand it as if from within. On a clear night look at the moon and the stars, spend time with the luminaries of the night; nothing exapands your soul like that. Out in the garden or field put your hand in the wet earth, take a handful of mud and play with it. Take a lump of clay and try to fashion something out of it, anything at all, however simple. Look at your hands when they are covered with loose clay; try to understand the shape of your hands without their natural colour – just the shape, with the uniform colour of clay – and see if the feeling you have corresponds with what you feel before great sculpture. Try to mingle with flowers, trees, grass and hay, talk to them and seek their fellowship. Search for the rhythm of life and growth around you, watch the fall of leaves, the sprouting of new shoots, the movements of winds and of waves. Swing with this rhythm, give yourself to it, float on it like a twig on a river, or a feather in the wind; let it take hold of you and carry you where it wills.

From the point of view of Franciscan spirituality or Franciscan training I consider exercises of this kind to be as important as any of the spiritual exercises given in the books. But while you do these things, don't let yourself be seen by people who do not understand this sort of thing; with great charity they might arrange to have you put away in an institution and go and pray for you. You have to become a bit of a fool – and if you think that is too much of a price to pay, it might just possibly be that you are a little too large for the eye of the needle.

Beyond the Needle's Eye

But if you can manage to scrape through that eye, what is on the other side can be a rewarding experience. It might take a little time, but slowly, very slowly, you will begin to understand the cosmic fellowship of Francis. Genuine wood with its face, its thickness, its inner texture, its way of responding to steel or to heat or cold, its weight and its character will then invite you to go deeper than its polished surface and meet its soul. Stone, metal, glass, wool – each material will speak a language of its own. The sound of a bell will fall on your ear-drums as the voice of your Sister Bronze; in the voices of fire and of water you will recognize the masculine throat of a brother and the high soprano of a sister. You will learn that just like people, things too have not only character, but temperaments as well; you will understand the moods of the elements. Things thus met in their totality will come to you with a beauty that goes beyond the senses.

Slowly you will begin to understand a new dimension of the prayer of Francis, and you will also begin to taste the sweetness of this prayer of cosmic brotherhood. Then you will begin to understand why this man was like that, and why he did the things he did. You will see too why he keeps tugging at your heart-strings and what made Masseo say to him, "Why after you? Why after you? Why does the whole world run after you?"

If Francis of Assisi can take charge of our attitudes toward matter in this way, we shall find that as a consummate artist he will transform all of creation into vehicles of the spirit for us, and he will enable us to enflesh the Word in everything we touch. Not only nature as it came from God's hands, but man-made objects too will come to us as having a life of their own, and claiming us for brothers and sisters. Beginning with simple and everyday things like a pin, a rubber band, a paper-clip, a pair of scissors, a fork, and going on to more complicated ones like a bicycle, a clock, a sewing machine, and on to the most sophisticated electronic equipment, everything will become for us a source not only of endless wonderment and joy, but of God-experience, as long as they are true to themselves and do not cheat nature. A keenness for authenticity is the key to a great happening indeed within.

If Francis were to come back today he would marvel at the ball-point pen, go crazy over the pocket calculator and hit the roof for sheer wonder at the mission to outer space. He would listen with incredulous enchantment to quadraphonic stereo, but after that would listen with equal enchantment to the village brass-band or to a team of drummers. After watching television with goggle-eyed wonder he would still be able to watch with fascination the flame of a candle and talk to Brother Fire with the old familiarity, or watch the dew-drop on the grass and see the Pleiades and Orion enshrined in it.

Porta Moiano,
Assisi

7 Of Stories And Dreams

"They should always have this writing with them together with the Rule, and in the chapters they hold, when they read the Rule they should read these words also."
— The Testament of Saint Francis

LYING ON HIS DEATH-BED, Francis of Assisi entertained the dream that his Rule and his Testament, the two documents that held so much of his blood, sweat and tears, would always mean something special to his followers. He visualized that the men and women who would follow him for all ages would come together in small groups from time to time to sit down and listen together to his words, to be bonded in one and carried in spirit to the time and place where the new vision the Lord revealed to him unfolded as a story.

The Rule was for him the crystallization of this story and the shrine of his vision and experience, not a piece of legislation. That is why he wrote (in the Rule of 1221), "Kissing their feet I beg them all to love, observe and treasure this Rule." To observe the Rule was not enough; it had to be loved and treasured as well. What Francis wanted was not obedient servants, but brothers and sharers in his vision.

What he meant by "love and treasure" he had described in an earlier passage where he wrote, "In the name of the Lord I beg all my brothers to learn the sense and purport of all that is written down in this way of life for the salvation of our souls, and to call it to mind again and again." To learn the meaning of the text of the Rule was the first and most obvious thing, but there was a second part, typical of

Francis: he wanted it to be read and "called to mind again and again."

He was not the kind of legalist who would have meant by "the Rule" just the official and final *Regula Bullata*. The Rule was for him the summary of his way of life, therefore the earlier Rules and all that led to its formulation were part of it. It also had a context, and the context was the story. As he approached his death, lying for days on end in that bed, he realized how important was that story. Frame by frame, as it were, it all passed before his eyes, beginning with that first dream when he was twenty-two and still "in sin", and going through his sojourn with the lepers and the repairing of the churches, the coming of the brothers, their groping together for a way of life, their struggle with the powers within and the powers without, and the hand of the Lord leading them through all these. He lived through them all again in his mind and saw how irreplaceable were stories. No explanations or analyses could capture the soul of the vision as it lived in the narratives. The Rule did capture it in a way, but only in a way; there was a large part of it that was still too mobile and too hazy to be captured in anything but stories. So just a few days before the end, with his strength and his voice already failing, Francis called for his writer and dictated his last Will and Testament.

In it with the intuition of a dying man he told his story, went back over the whole adventure and picked out the key moments and turning points – the lepers, the churches, the Eucharist, the brothers, community, prayer, poverty, work, his reverence for priests and for God's word – he strung all these up on the thread of the Lord's initiative . . . "the Lord led me, . . . the Lord gave me, . . . the Lord showed me" and then rounded them off with a few words of encouragement and counsel.

Looking into the past he recalled the wonders the Lord had done for him – narrated a story – and looking into the future he admonished and counselled his friars – projected a dream. This double action of looking back and forward in the final presentation of his vision shows how, intuitively, Francis grasped the time-bound, durational and dynamic aspect of his vocation and charism. That was the world in which he lived so intensely during those days, as can be seen in that other dying statement of his – almost a perfect summary of his Testament – "My brothers, I have done my part; may Christ teach you what is yours."

Now this Testament he places side by side with his Rule and begs that the two be read together and that they may be "called to mind again and again." It is not enough to analyze and study them; they should be often listened to and meditated upon.

Franciscans of earlier times frequently read in community not only the Rule and the Testament, but stories from the life of Saint Francis. It was for this purpose that Celano and Bonaventure wrote their *Legenda* (which means "passages for reading out"). Celano even wrote a book of readings specifically "for use in choir" during the Divine Office.

That wise teacher, Franciscan Tradition, devised various ways of ensuring that the study of the Rule and the Testament would not stop at the desk and the classroom; among them was the reading of these documents in common at every chapter and regularly in the refectory or other places where the friars met. In modern times these and similar customs have had to be dropped in many places. Perhaps there were good reasons for this: times have changed, lifestyles have changed, work-patterns have changed. But it would be a pity if the reasoning for the changes went along the following lines: "We all know what these texts contain; what is the use of reading them in public again and again? Those who want can read them privately. The important thing, after all, is that we observe the Rule." If we found ourselves at home with such reasoning, it would be an indication that we were blind to some enriching values of life.

Types of Reading

There are different kinds of reading. For many of us one of the important happenings of the day is the newspaper. We make a grab for it, but once we have got hold of it, within twenty minutes or so it becomes a useless thing. We have read what was in it and, unless there were some special reason, would not want to read it again.

There is a second category of reading material, the kind that after we have read once, we might require again, because all the information or literary pleasure contained in it has not been absorbed. That is the kind of material we store, the books we keep in the library and read again.

There is a third kind. It consists mostly of the stories, poems and what could be called wisdom material, that form the basis of a community's existing together. The reading and re-reading of these, as well as the method of this reading, follow quite different dynamics.

Stories

When a group of friends meet, they like to tell stories of their old escapades. Friends are people who have created stories together and share a past and enjoy telling them again. The function of this story-telling is not to inform one another, but to re-live the past and touch the ground of their fellowship again. There is something of ritual about it. The archaism and repetition are accepted as relevant. If it is a new story (news story) you may tell it only once, but if it is an old and well-known story of this nature, you may repeat it meaningfully again and again.

Listening Together

A group of people sitting together, with one person reading out a narrative that concerns them all in depth, and the rest listening to it with attention is an activity where great power is at work. It is more than a relic of the days when books were expensive and few could read. It is a celebration of common ground. The dead word of the book is brought alive by the reader. He transforms the flat and motionless pattern of ink on paper into living vibrations filling the hall and reaching through the ears into the minds and hearts of all present. It gathers them all up into a celebrating body, with their spirits touching one another's and being cemented together by this group activity. From being a pattern on paper the word is clothed with living sound and subjected to time and space and turned into an event with a beginning and an end. With the coming of movement and duration the word becomes word in the full sense – the dynamic reaching out between two intelligent termini. It binds the reader and the listeners together and carries them into the past and makes them joint participants in their root stories. You read privately for information and study, you read in public for celebration and for ritual absorption into the story.

The Christian Community is based on a collection of stories, poems and wise sayings called the Bible. When Christians come together they re-tell these and thus reach down to the roots of their fellowship and unite themselves closer to each other and to the ground of their togetherness. The Divine Office of the Church is precisely this kind of re-telling. The greatest religious act performed by Christians, the Eucharist, always contains the re-telling of these stories, and is itself in its essence the re-telling and re-living of the central happening that has fashioned them into a body of people.

The stories that bind us together as Franciscans and form the basis of our Franciscan existence are the stories concerning Saint Francis and the early friars. It was in these stories, and not in a series of statements or principles, that God revealed to Francis this new way of being Christian. Francis and his companions had to "wrestle all night" with this revelation in

109

order to give it flesh in their historical setting. They had to grope too and find God's will the hard way. They had to struggle with it in the situations of their times in order to master it. Thus the Franciscan vision was played out in a historical and durational manner.

This process is still ongoing. If we want to translate this vision for our times and situations, what we have to do is not merely to analyze the manner in which they did it, come to the root principles and methods and then after a study of our own times and problems, apply those principles and reach conclusions on how we may live our vocation. We have to go farther. What we have to do is to enter into their story. By ritual and fantasy, and the use of our senses and imagination as well as our intellect we have to become participants in their story and then wrestle with that same vision in our own dark night and mingle our story with theirs and our dream with theirs. Thus our story, combined with that of the early friars and of Francis, can ultimately be combined with the story of Jesus. Only then can our distinctly Franciscan vision as part of the historical and ongoing working out of the Christian vision through the ages be meaningfully realized.

Rituals for Stories

We shall always need rituals to keep in touch with the springs of our fellowship. That is why, while some of our rituals, which might have been borrowed from monastic usage, have disappeared, others have been taking their place. Such are group masses and para-liturgies, which accompany many of our important events. More of such rituals – with a good bit of story-telling in them – will have to be evolved as time goes on, to keep us from becoming pious businessmen and our chapters from turning into Governing Body Meetings.

It is beauty that has to keep us from ossifying in that way.

We Franciscans are fortunate in that the life of Saint Francis is not only strewn and splattered with stories, but they are all of them beautiful. Every one of them is a song.

Some of them may be disturbing, some queer or illogical. They refuse to be ordered and neatly stacked together like books on a shelf. They are too much like the Gospel stories, vibrant and volatile. And like them too, they are all of them piercingly beautiful.

We need beauty around us to grow. Just as a child cannot grow into maturity unless he is surrounded by smiles, so too, a group of religious cannot grow into the fullness of all the possibilities in them, unless they are surrounded by beautiful stories.

Dreams

"When you read the Rule, read these words also", said the dying Francis.

We might paraphrase it this way:

I know, my sons and daughters, that times will change. There will be new cultures, new pressures, new needs. And I know also that as long as the world holds together there will be Brothers and Sisters who believe in me. They will come together from time to time to study the Rule and my ideals, and seriously to discuss how to live them out in their own situations.

But I would like to beg for one more thing. When you come together to study the Rule and my vision in this way, please do not forget the stories that lie behind them. Read them too, and become my contemporaries. Read them often, together.

That is why in this last Will and Testament of mine I have tried to tell my story, in my own way and as far as I can remember.

I have also added a few words of advice and encouragement for you.

Those are my dreams for you.
I want my dreams to become your stories,
and my stories to touch off your dreams.
Let them make you dream dreams of your own.
Never let go of dreams, my children,
never let go of dreams.
And if you dream,
and cherish your dreams,
they will turn into stories.
Believe me, they will –
not the way a plan develops into a house,
but the way
a rose-bud in the sunshine
grows and blooms into a rose
with warmth from above
and power from within.

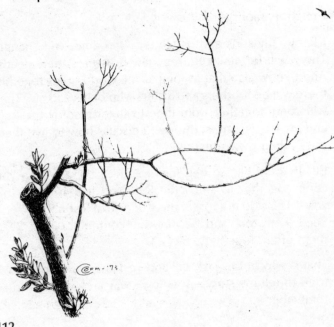

8 The One Master

A FTER SPENDING some months in Assissi I was on my way back to India and was stopping over in the Holy Land. But in my heart the Holy Land was not a mere stopover, it was the climax of my pilgrimage. The miles and miles of Franciscan paths I had walked in Italy would lead nowhere if they did not lead to the paths where Jesus had walked.

Literally Francis had walked the paths of the Holy Land. From eight centuries away I wanted to walk behind him, tracing the footprints of our common Master.

In Rome I boarded a 'plane for Tel-Aviv. Next to me there came and sat an elderly couple. I was glad to find them to be Americans, after all those months of *Italiano* in my ears all day long. He was a man of few words, but she more than made up for that. After some preliminaries she told me they were Jews and were on their first pilgrimage to Israel. She described in detail how they had saved all their lives for this trip and now, with all their children settled in life, were fulfilling their life-long ambition. They were excitedly looking forward to setting foot on the land of Abraham, Isaac and Jacob. Then she asked me what I was. "I am a Catholic priest", I answered. "Oh, Catholic", she said, "I was brought up in a Catholic town", and gave its name, which I have forgotten. "We were the only non-Catholics there and so had to go to the Catholic school. The children began calling us Jews 'Christ-killers'. I didn't know what that meant. So I went home crying to my father and said, 'Daddy, they are calling us Christ-killers. What does that mean? Who

113

is this Christ?' And my father answered, 'Jesus Christ is the man who has made everything so difficult for us Jews.'"

If till then I had spoken little, after that I spoke less than little. I had this big sentence to chew on and to ruminate: Jesus Christ is the man who has made everything so difficult for us Jews. I sat there quietly and kept repeating to myself over and over again, "Yes, Jesus Christ is the man who has made everything so difficult for all of us." If it weren't for Christ, things would be so different and life would be so easy. But at every turn of the road, there he stands saying: "That is not good enough, you can do better."

And the worst part of it is that in throwing down his gauntlet, this most demanding of challengers shows the utmost respect for your freedom with the terrible irony of those three words, "If anyone wishes" . . . (Matt. 16:24) and keeps on offering this freedom all along the line – "Would you also go away?" (John 6:67). Everywhere I walked during that pilgrimage – in the narrow, crowded streets of Jerusalem, the grounds of the Temple, the rock of Calvary, the open roads of Galilee, the shores of the Sea of Gennesareth – everywhere those words of the Jewish lady kept haunting me, ". . . the man who has made everything so difficult . . ." and as the phrase kept repeating itself, it began to shine, and I could not help adding, "and so beautiful."

The Guide

What made this whole experience what it was for me was the fact that I had Francis of Assisi as guide and companion on my journey. And this not merely because he had physically walked those roads before me, but because he had done so in metaphor as well. The meaning he holds for me is coherent only in the context of a Christ-experience. Francis is Francis because he took up, as no one ever did, the difficult challenge of Christ and found it, as no one ever did, to be beautiful, the bitter to be sweet. Any follower of Francis can make sense of the whole thing only by seeing Francis' life as a further challenge and companionship in the following of this Man, who keeps making everything so difficult . . . and so beautiful.

Francis was thus my companion on this journey through the Holy Land, my fellow-traveller, fellow-seeker and fellow-disciple. The friary where I stayed most of the time in Jerusalem was named after the Holy Saviour and had the simple (and for me not without meaning) address: No 1, Saint Francis Street. It is the street that goes on and becomes the Way of the Cross. Every Friday the Franciscan friars conduct the Stations there leading a large crowd of people along the path where the barefooted Jesus walked to his death carrying his cross, and where many large tear-drops have fallen from the face of Francis.

The special place that the Holy Land held in the mind and spirituality of Saint Francis was part of his whole outlook on life and approach to God. He wanted "to see with my own bodily eyes the destitution of the Child born in Bethlehem . . ." He wanted his senses and fantasy to be part of his worship; it was only through them that he could gather the whole of creation in his journey to God. He was an "audio-visual" man long before the modern age of the media. This aspect of Francis that I find most captivating is what I have been trying to explore all along.

Talking of the Eucharist, Francis said: "In this world I cannot see the most high Son of God with my own eyes, except for his most holy Body and Blood." He was not unaware of the fact that even in the Eucharist we do not see the Body and Blood of Christ, but only bread and wine. In the Holy Land anyway, he could see with his own eyes the spot where Jesus was born, the paths where he walked, the rock on which he hung on the cross, the tomb that he broke out of. With his hands he could play with the waves on the Sea of

Galilee and fondle the wild flowers of the field that Jesus placed above King Solomon, he could hear the sparrows that were all counted and kept track of by the Father in heaven, he could walk down from Jerusalem to Emmaus with the two dispirited disciples and be joined by the Master himself, in Bethany he could sit with Mary at those hallowed feet and drink in the divine words.

In a sense he made the whole world a Holy Land. Whatever he could see, touch, hear, smell or taste bore the marks of Jesus and was part of his pilgrimage to God.

The Francis of People

Searching for the Francis of aesthetics, as I have been trying to, one would have to be blind to miss the Francis of people. His God dwelt not in the mountains and forests alone, but in the villages as well, not in fire and water alone, but in faces and wrinkled hands as well, and in the personalities behind the faces and hands. If the fascination of Francis and of the Franciscan Order through the centuries for the Holy Land can be seen as a symbol of the sense aspect, or "audio-visual" bent of his spirituality, equally symbolic could be the following story.

In the time of Pope Pius XI, the General of a large and powerful group of men religious, who was a personal friend of the pope, once spoke to him about how the Franciscans were having custody of most of the important sanctuaries in the Holy Land and asked that some of them be given to his men. The pope promised to consider it. The Franciscan General, Leonardo Bello, heard of it and went to see the pope. He told him how the friars through the centuries had acquired, built up and guarded the shrines and ministered to the people, and showed him a list of two thousand friars who had given their lives serving the sick during an epidemic of plague there. The pope looked at the list and told him the friars could carry on.

That list of dead friars is as much part of the Franciscan approach to God in Christ. For all his joy in colours and shapes and sounds, Francis was not the kind of man who could forget that the God of the Christians is a God of people. In fact his singular compassion for the suffering Christ and his longing to be a participant in that suffering had its roots in his attitudes towards people. He went to Christ through people.

Empathy

One of the first glimpses we get of the adolescent Francis is that of a salesman, and a good one. People loved dealing with him, we are told, because of his pleasant manners, "his almost superhuman readiness to oblige and his generosity which exceeded his means."[1] One of the natural foundations that God laid in the making of the saint was this gift for compassion. He had an extraordinary capacity to feel with others. This capacity is the first requirement for love. To love is not to think with the other, or to help the other, but first to feel with and into the other.

He was always kind to beggars. A lot of people are, because that is a good salve for consciences laden with luxury. But his kindness was different. Once in a moment of absent-mindedness he turned a beggar away from his shop. Most people would have told their conscience they would try to be careful next time. But when Francis realized the slip, his first thought was, "What does it feel like to be turned away?" If you put yourself in the shoes of the other man like that, there is only one thing you can do. Francis left the shop and ran after the man. We do not know how long he had to run and search before he found him, but in the narrow, twisted and steep lanes of Assisi if you can stop for a while and "listen" you can still hear the swish of his robes and his panting as he rushed from corner to corner looking to right and to left till he found the man and showered him with alms and apologies.

117

It was some time after this that in Rome he saw a large number of beggars at the door of St Peter's Basilica. He gave them all the money he had, and then the old question started coming back to him, "What does it feel like to be a beggar, to be dependent on others, to have people turn their backs on you?" An impish desire to try it out came upon him. After all, no one knew him in this place. He exchanged clothes with a beggar for a day, literally got into his shoes – and also his baggy trousers, stinking coat and greasy hat. St Peter's was a much smaller church then than it is now, but somewhere in the middle of its nave now if you pause for a while under the gigantic arches, you might be literally standing where Francis stood all day and begged, and got his first taste of poverty.

This capacity of Francis to "feel into" others, to get under their skin, shines out nowhere brighter than in his encounter with the leper – that absolutely sublime and devastatingly powerful incident in his life. It is not merely the obvious forcefulness of the facts, or the heroism it called for from a man of his delicate upbringing, but there is a mystical dimension to it, a poetic aura, a dramatic finish and a wealth of symbolism. Years later, on his deathbed, Francis was to recall it in his *Testament* as the most momentous turning point in his life, which spun his world upside down, making all that was bitter sweet and sweet bitter. He recalled it humbly and unpretentiously in somewhat generalized terms and as something the Lord did to him in which he received rather than gave.

For the pilgrim in Assisi today there is something providential and fortunate about this story: no one knows where it happened. If they did, they would have gone and built a large basilica over it, with a parking lot and half a dozen souvenir shops and cafeterias. In the middle of the church would be a bronze or marble statue to make sure that no prayerful use of fantasy would ever be made there.

But now, any of the dozens of dusty paths in the plains around Assisi could have been that road. You can wander there all alone and in the shadow of any of those trees you can pause and see our young hero. He comes riding along on his horse with not a care in the world, his damask mantle and tinsel cap catching the morning sun. Suddenly he gives a tug at the reins and stops. His nostrils have caught a stench. Looking up he sees before him the threat of his life, a leper. He is about to throw a coin and turn the horse aside, when the old question pulls at his sleeve: "What does it mean to be a leper? How does the world look from his point of view? What does it mean to be avoided by everyone, to have no friends in the world?" The threat of his life becomes now the challenge of his life. The next moment he is down from the horse. Putting his arms around the man he kisses that face.

I think that is the moment the Franciscan event happened in the history of the world. In the dust of that nameless road and under that Italian sun Francis embraced all humankind, with not a word spoken.

Then with the air of one who has done nothing special he jumps back on his horse and comes away, bearing on his head, and on the heads of all of us his sons and daughters to the end of time, the blessing of a leper . . . of the One despised and rejected, who makes everything so difficult . . . and so beautiful.

This story is quite central and in a way all-inclusive. But there are many more incidents in his life that show him as a man who could enter into the feelings of others. Like that of the novice who cried out at night of hunger. Or that of the sick brother with whom he ate grapes.

But there is one that could be re-told here. Leo, his friend and confessor, was the only brother allowed to be with Francis during his stay on the mountain top of La Verna. He prized the friendship and confidence of Francis above

119

everything in the world. But after the Stigmata, he noticed that Francis was beginning to be more and more withdrawn, more and more lost in God. What place did he, Leo, have in Francis' affections? For days he brooded over the sad spectre of estrangement haunting his friendship. What was he to do? If it was anything else that was troubling his soul he could have spoken to Francis about it, but this? If only he could get some sign of Francis' love! Slowly his longing began to take definite shape in his mind, though more in the form of a wild day-dream that would never materialize. What he would like to have from Francis was a written assurance that Leo did matter to him. And if he had such a document in his hand, how he would treasure it! He would carry it on his person, next to his heart to his dying day. But . . . those were castles in the air; there was no point in building them up, only to be blown away in the wind. Suddenly he hears a voice. Yes, it is Francis calling him. "Leo, Brother Leo, . . . please bring me a piece of parchment and your writing material." Leo makes a grab for them and rushes up. There with his wounded hand Francis writes on one side of the parchment the praises of God that have been welling up in his heart, and on the other a personal, autographed blessing for Leo, with a bit of playful doodling – his signature, the letter Tau, or T, resembling a cross, placed on something that could be Leo's head, or Mount Calvary, or both.

Both Celano and Bonaventure attribute Francis' knowledge of Leo's desire to the inspiration of the Holy Spirit. But we need not see a miracle in this. The Spirit showed it to him through his delicate sensitivity to the needs of others.

It was many years before Leo died. And when they laid out his body they found a pocket stitched into his habit next to his heart. In it was this document folded in four. You can see it today in the Basilica of Saint Francis in Assisi, still bearing the sweat and dirt of Leo's body – this piece of parchment which is a symbol of what life in God meant to Francis: on the one side pure praise of God, and on the other concern for a worried brother.

This concern for others and sensitivity to their needs was the result of Grace building on natural gifts. Francis was the sort of man whose attitude toward the suffering or comfort of others was the opposite of ours. When we see someone suffering, even if we sympathize, we say under our breath: "Thank goodness I am not in that position". When we see a man having a good time we say: "I wish I were like that". But when Francis saw a man suffering he could enter into his personality and suffer with him, and when he saw a well-dressed man (garments were a sign of wealth and social standing much more in his time than they are in ours), he could accept him without envy or contempt and go on "rather to judge and despise himself".

Constantly taking upon himself the sorrows of others and seeing the world from their point of view, Francis came to enter more fully into the personality of Christ. For Christ is God taking upon himself our sorrows and seeing the world from our point of view.

If Christ is our way to God, then people are our way to Christ. Francis took that way. He was not led to people through Christ, as some try to be, who look upon other people as objects for practising their love of God on. Francis took people seriously, as being important in themselves (as indeed he took everything else). In sharing their sorrows he discovered he was sharing the sorrows of Christ. Thus he came to see his own sorrows as part of the sorrows of all mankind, which are the sorrows of Christ.

It was this capacity for compassion that made this man who so loved life and laughter to long for suffering and seek after it almost as if he were a masochist. The only reaction he could find in his heart to the passion of Christ was to seek for a share in it.

121

The Demand

The Christ that he thus came to understand was not a soft comforter, but the most demanding, though the gentlest, of masters. In an age such as ours, the eternal attraction of Christ has gathered around him as varied a crowd of seekers and admirers as there ever was, each one looking from his own angle and seeing Christ as the superstar, the revolutionary, the liberator, the communist, the hippie, the teacher, the healer, the saviour, the consoler. Francis reminds us that in whatever way we see Christ, we shall miss the whole point of him if we do not see him primarily as a *demand*, as one who makes everything difficult. To look on Christ in a purely human manner was a sin according to Francis; he must be seen in the spirit. To see Christ in the spirit is to see him as God on earth, as Emmanuel.

The first meaning of Jesus Christ is that we are important to God, and that we are accepted as we are. The second, that being thus God's children places demands on us.

Recounting how Francis enacted the Christmas scene in Greccio, Celano tells us that a certain virtuous man present there had a vision in which he saw a sleeping child whom the saint took in his arms and woke from sleep. Bonaventure gives his name as John. He could well have been Francis' friend Sir John who had worked all day preparing the crib and the altar and making all the arrangements for the dramatic celebration. We can forgive John if he dozed off during the sermon and dreamt this scene, for dreams have a way of going straight to the heart of the matter and summing up a situation in symbols. Celano points out this meaning to us: "This vision was not unfitting, for the Child Jesus had been forgotten in the hearts of many; but by the working of his grace he was brought to life again through his servant Saint Francis."

What happened high up in that mountain village of Greccio

has been much romanticized. Francis set up a stable with live beasts and a wooden doll in a crib and had the whole countryside come up with torches and lanterns on Christmas night to celebrate mass by the cave. What he did there was more than provide ideas for our Christmas decoration or pose for our greeting cards. His idea was "to call to mind the little Child who was born in Bethlehem and set before our bodily eyes in some way how he was laid in a manger and how he rested where he was placed on the straw, with the ox and the ass standing by." Besides being a joyful celebration of God's coming among us, or rather, precisely by being a celebration, the whole scene is a questioning of our values, a challenge to our love of comfort. If Christ is "Emmanuel", he will be a demanding "God-with-us". For all its song, gaiety and celebration, Christmas is for Francis a time when God makes us uncomfortable in our silken clothes and soft beds – the way only a destitute infant can.

Francis' other favourite theme was the cross of Christ. It had appeared emblazoned on all the shields and banners that the castle of his first dream was hung with. On the day of his new birth to God, when before his earthly father and the Bishop and the whole populace of Assisi he stripped himself naked and was given a farmhand's smock, he took a piece of chalk and scrawled on it a large cross before wearing it. From that moment on, his one ambition was to scrawl that cross on his life. The final touch of this artistic work was given on Mount La Verna when God added the five wounds.

These wounds were not decorations. They were real wounds. They bled and required dressing. They were painful, inconvenient things to have around. And as such they were symbolic.

He asked for them, in a way, not realizing what he was going to get. Papini said, "When nature wants to punish the great for their greatness, she sends them disciples." When the burden of leadership began to weigh heavily on him, his prayer of petition began to zero down to two points. All he wanted for himself was as big a share as was humanly bearable in the sufferings of Christ, and in what gave meaning to it, his love. Jesus took him seriously enough to show him that what hurt him most in his passion was not being mocked by Herod, judged by Pilate, beaten and spat upon by the soldiers or carrying the cross and being nailed to it. What hurt him more than the insults and injuries from his enemies was his desertion by his friends. Francis had to go through that too. Slowly he found himself deserted by most of his friends. They became admirers, worshippers, but were no more friends prepared to stand by him and his vision. His relics became more important than his ideals. It was in this period of loneliness that he composed his Parable of Perfect Joy. In it, searching for perfect joy, he looks at all the most wonderful things that could happen to his Order, things that would make the heart of any founder leap for joy. Then, passing them all by, he finally finds it in being thrown out by his brothers in the cold and accepting all that without complaining, as his just share in the sufferings of Christ. Such an exquisite parable could have been written only by someone who had gone through it all in his heart. And then Christ led him deeper still, deeper into the abysmal darkness of the soul in which he had cried out on his cross: "My God, my God, why have you forsaken me?" He kept on making everything difficult for his servant, and only when at last he found him worthy, imprinted on him those five wounds.

Eucharist, The Summing Up

Having stressed the nativity and the passion of Christ, the beginning and the end of his human life, Francis had to make sure that the Christ he adored and embraced was not merely man, but God-with-us-as-Man. His instincts told him to keep far from the heresy of Arianism. To balance his stress on the humanity of Christ, Francis laid emphasis on another mystery, the Eucharist.

The Eucharist was for Francis the link between the two worlds, the guarantee that in his devotions the humanity of Christ, which he found so attractive, was one with his divinity. On the altar table all heaven and earth came together in a blinding fusion. In that blinding fusion too all the pains of life converged, melted, and turned into joy. Before it, all he could do was fall down and worship.

Writing to a General Chapter he said: "Kissing your feet with all the love I am capable of, I beg you to show the greatest possible reverence and honour for the most holy Body and Blood of our Lord Jesus Christ through whom all things, whether on the earth or in the heavens, have been brought to peace and reconciled with Almighty God." How much that meant to him can be seen from the fact that it churned up his fantasy to giving us images and stories with power to churn ours too. Being the dramatist he was, what he wrote on paper he had to act out in real life; he used to walk around the countryside with a broom in his hand and when he entered a church, if he found it untidy, would sweep it. There is a tiny church, in a tiny village called Nottiano lost in the woods on the other (Eastern) side of Mount Subasio, which Francis swept in this way, and which still stands. I found it to be the most moving of all the Franciscan places, because it has not yet been discovered by tourists, the approach to it being difficult.

There are no decorations in it, and nothing has been built around or near it. Being almost deserted, it has been barely maintained. There it stands in all its simplicity and ruggedness, very much as it must have in those days. You can still kneel there, on the stone paved floor and see Francis moving about, performing his humble liturgy of the broom.

Images of this sort call up other images. In Jerusalem the house where the first Eucharist took place is now owned by the Muslims. But they permit tourists to visit it, including the Upper Room of the Last Supper. Fortunately for me, the morning I went up to it there were hardly any tourists around, and I spent a long time in that room all alone, trying to recreate and live through all that had happened there. I realized that Francis must have stood there too, but what must have gone through his mind and heart I could not follow any more than a chicken could follow an eagle. But I could certainly visualize with what devotion he would have swept that floor.

All those impressions of the Upper Room and its neighbour-hood seem to form in my mind into a strange harmony with the Church of Nottiano and a lot of other churches. A piece of bread broken in that room and multiplied a billion billion times around the world, which I too hold in my hand every morning, is the centre and balancing point of the cosmos up to the outermost galaxy. Yet from that point every sparrow is important and not a single one falls dead without being taken note of.

Every morning when I break this bread and commune with all created universe and its uncreated centre, the Lord Jesus, I thank him for the man who has taught me most about him and his values, and keeps deepening and broadening that vision every day, Francis of Assisi. Endowed by nature with an extraordinary sense for the dramatic and for all things earthy, and a deep intuition into their essences, as well as a heart that naturally went out to other people in sympathy, Francis spent all his life celebrating and searching. He called out to the birds, mountains and rivers and to the stars of heaven to celebrate with him, and in compassion reached out to all who shared his human condition, but especially to those whose lives were broken, wasted and lost. Touching the lowest layer of their humanity, he found there another humanity, also broken, wasted and lost.

Embracing it he found that around that point circled the stars of heaven and the mountains, rivers and birds he had befriended, and that, concentrated on that point, was unspeakable pain and unspeakable joy, calling out to all who would listen, and offering to take their lives too, and make everything difficult, and everything beautiful.

The village church of Nottiano

References

Chapter 1

1. The reference here is to the old Cimabue in San Francesco. It does not exist any more. As a result of a "restoration" undertaken in 1972 or 1973, there stands in its place now a younger Francis, with much less character and power. All we have of the other one now are old prints. Our cover drawing is based on it.
2. M. Muggeridge, *Jesus Rediscovered* (London: Collins/Fontana, 1969), pp. 109, 204.
3. F. Timmermans, *The Perfect Joy of St Francis*, tr. R. Brown (New York: Doubleday/Image Books, 1955); L. de Wohl, *Francis of Assisi* (original title: *The Joyful Beggar*. New York: Popular Library, 1960); M. Bodo, *Francis: The Journey and the Dream* (Cincinnati: St Anthony Messenger Press, 1972); *Clare, a Light in the Garden* (Cincinnati, 1979); *Juniper, Friend of Francis, Fool of God* (Cincinnati, 1983); *Tales of St Francis* (New York: Doubleday, 1986).
4. M. Muggeridge, *Jesus, the Man who Lives*, (London: Collins/Fontana, 1976), p. 38.
5. E. Doyle OFM, *Francis and the Song of Brotherhood* (London: Allen & Unwin, 1980), p. 74.
6. See S. Tugwell OP, *St Dominic and the Order of Preachers* (London: Catholic Truth Society, 1981), p. 1.
7. *Mirror of Perfection*, 68.

Chapter 6

1. N. Kazantzakis, *Saint Francis* (New York: Ballantine Books, 1966), p. 7.
2. M. Muggeridge, *Jesus, the Man who Lives*, p. 30.

Chapter 8

1. St Bonaventure, *Legenda Major*, I, 1.

NOTE

The original edition of *A New Kind of Fool* is a landscape-format book, 10¼" × 7¼", of 312 pages, containing, in addition to the material used in this edition, verse meditations, colour and black and white photographs and more drawings by the author, plus a selection of songs with music by the author. It is avalable from: Amruthavani, PB 1588, Secunderabad 500 003, India.